AN AGE OF SAINTS

Also published by Llanerch:

SYMBOLISM OF THE CELTIC CROSS by Derek Bryce, with
drawings by J. Romilly Allen and others.

THE TOMBS OF THE KINGS: AN IONA BOOK OF THE
DEAD by John Marsden.

THE GODODDIN OF ANEIRIN translated by Steve Short.

TALIESIN POEMS translated by Meirion Pennar.

THE BLACK BOOK OF CARMARTHEN translated by
Meirion Pennar.

THE AGE OF THE SAINTS IN CORNWALL by W. C.
Borlase.

LIVES AND LEGENDS OF ST. BRENDAN THE VOYAGER
edited by Denis O'Donaghue.

THE LIFE OF ST. COLUMBAN by Jonas the Monk,
translated by D. C. Munro.

THE ADORNMENT OF THE SPIRITUAL MARRIAGE, THE
SPARKLING STONE, THE BOOK OF SUPREME TRUTH by
Jan Ruysbroeck, English translation edited by Evelyn
Underhill.

ANGLO-SAXON RELIGIOUS VERSE ALLEGORIES
translated by Louis Rodrigues.

For a complete list of c.200 small-press editions and
facsimile reprints, history, folklore, spirituality, etc., write to
LLANERCH PUBLISHERS, Felinfach, Lampeter,
Cardiganshire, SA48 8PJ.

AN AGE OF SAINTS

Its relevance for us today

Chalwyn James

The Celtic parts of Britain are by far the poorer but they are also the most beautiful, and their poverty has enabled them to retain wider vision, the timeless sense of romance and the spiritual outlook denied to the busier and more prosperous communities.

Nora Chadwick

Llanerch

Illustrations by Bryan Barton from photographs by the author.

Typeset by Kenneth Burnley in Irby, Wirral, Cheshire.

Printed and published by Llanerch Enterprises, Felinfach,
Lampeter, Dyfed, Wales SA48 8PJ.

Reprinted with minor revisions 1997.

ISBN 1 86143 020 5

Contents

Illustrations

Preface

If asked the question which was Britain's greatest age many might reflect on the events of the last four centuries. These would include a long and painful Reformation eventually leading in the late 17th century to the sudden emergence of a new age of enlightenment and reason. Within a very few years of the final expulsion of the Catholic Stuarts from the English throne came, for example, the major works of Locke and Newton, the Act of Toleration, and the lapsing of the Licensing Acts leading to freedom of the press. It was as if a bottle, previously corked by dogma, established church, and blinkered tradition, had suddenly exploded. The vestiges of a medieval cosmos were scattered to the wind. The exact opposite, incidentally, was happening in France with the vindictive revocation of the Edict of Nantes in 1685. Following this Britain opened her shores to the industrious Huguenots and benefitted enormously from their skills.

All this helped to prepare a new and fertile seedbed that in turn nurtured the birth and growth of the industrial revolution which was centred in Britain in the 18th century. This revolution was a unique step in human history. It was predicated on a fortunate coincidence of natural resources, on capital amassed from wool and weaving and from slave labour in the British colonies of the Americas, on human ingenuity including Abraham Darby's innovative smelting of iron ore with coke, the increasingly efficient steam engines of Newcomen and Watt, and the uses of machinery particularly in transportation and in the textile industry, and on the beginnings of the factory system of manufacture. As a result, the 19th century certainly witnessed greatly increased wealth (for some), the expansion of trade, and the fruition and trappings of a great empire.

The above is undeniably true. But, as the 20th century draws to a close, elements of stagnation if not decline are already evident. And I would prophesy that historians writing, let us say, two hundred years from now (if there be any) will recognise the industrial revolution and its associated developments, now of course with worldwide ramifications, to have been so obviously unsustainable in terms of Earth's natural resources that they will wonder how we could ever have blithely assumed otherwise. Furthermore, these same future historians might well conclude Britain's greater contribution to world history to have been a spiritual one and of a much earlier date: the "Age of Saints".

I suffered a conventional English education in which not a word was uttered of the so-called Dark Ages, apart from a mention of Alfred's lack of expertise in baking. Rather, there was an indecent rush from the year 410 A.D. to 1066 and all that. Let me try, belatedly, to rectify part of this omission with, as Michelin would say, un peu d'histoire. We shall witness an improbable, indeed amazing, story of human endeavour and achievement in the face of hardship and with minimal resources, a story moreover always remaining in sure touch with Nature and the psychic roots of humankind, a story most apposite to our own troubled times and, I have come to believe, a possible source of inspiration for our uncertain future.

I   EUROPE'S CELTIC FRINGE

The Age of Saints comprises roughly the mid-5th to mid-7th centuries A.D., a period coincident with the darkest of the Dark Ages in England itself. The Saints were Celtic pastors and monks, a significant number of them itinerant and missionary. Their activities were centred first in the extreme western fringes of the British Isles, namely, Wales, Cornwall, Strathclyde and, most importantly, Ireland. To these localities should certainly be added Brittany and, later and significantly, the islands and seaboard of southwestern Scotland.

Christian influences first came to the British Isles from the continent of Europe during the time of the mid to late Roman Empire. Then followed, in these far western areas mentioned above, a period of development in some degree of isolation. This led to a geographically distinct and eventually distinctive branch of Christianity that has come to be known as the Celtic Church. Its achievements, as we shall see, were outstanding – amazingly so when one considers the relative paucity of natural resources available to the societies where it flourished. Eventually, it was to bring about a decisive end to the Dark Ages in Britain, and to become the major contributor to Christian civilisation in western Europe.

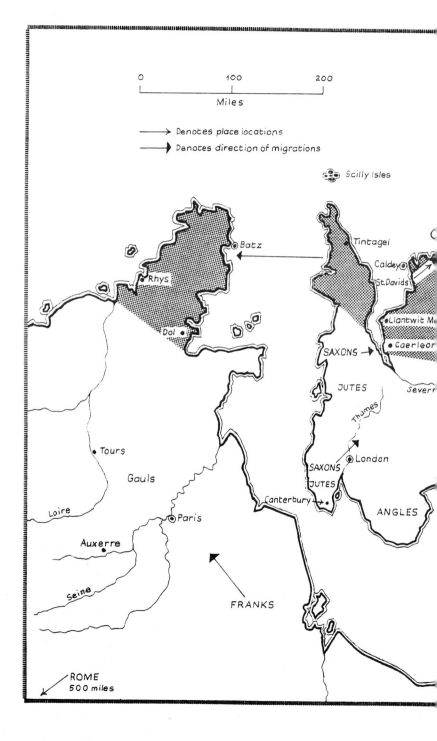

Scilly Isles

Batz

Tintagel

Caldey

St.Davids

Rhys

Llantwit M.

Dol

Caerleon

SAXONS →

JUTES

Severn

Thames

Tours

Gauls

SAXONS

London

JUTES

Loire

Canterbury →

ANGLES

Paris

Auxerre

Seine

FRANKS

ROME
500 miles

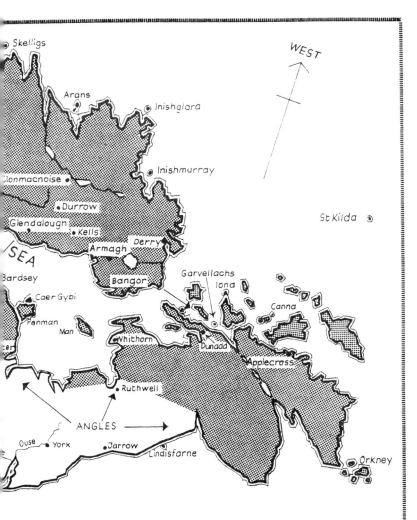

EUROPE'S CELTIC FRINGE

TERRITORY HELD BY NATIVE BRITISH PEOPLES DURING THE

AGE OF SAINTS IS SHOWN STIPPLED

Here we should perhaps digress and consider what is meant by the term Celtic. The "Keltoi" peoples were first described in writing in some detail by classical writers of Greece and Italy, notably by Poseidonius of Apamaea, who had travelled extensively among the Celts and wrote about them c.80 B.C. They comprised a large and diverse group of tribal peoples inhabiting at that time most of Europe north of the Alps and extending as far east as Galatia in Asia Minor (where Paul wrote an epistle to them). They were warlike; indeed, they had sacked Rome itself in 390 B.C. and Delphi in 279 B.C. They never built substantial cities – the traditional foci of high civilisations. Neither did they possess a written language. Nevertheless, they were not without culture, extremely extensive oral traditions, many artisan skills, and some towns, among the earliest in Europe. Their earlier towns mainly comprised those associated with the Hallstadt culture, based on salt mining from about the 8th century B.C. onwards in Austria, and coincident with the beginning of the Iron Age in Europe. By the first century B.C., some sixty sizable Celtic earthen-walled towns, "oppida", in western Europe included the five that the Romans found when they came to Britain, namely, Canterbury, Colchester, Silchester, St. Albans, and Braughing (in addition to numerous hill forts). Centres such as these housed chieftains and their retinues, metal-workers, carpenters, wheelwrights and numerous other artisans, together with traders. Celtic metalwork in bronze, gold, and iron had become outstanding and distinctive by the time of the La Tène culture from about the fourth century B.C. onwards. It produced a wide range of weapons, utensils and ornaments that

4

included swords, scabbards, shields, harness pieces, chariot fittings, hearthware, pins, torcs, and mirrors.

The main concentration of Celtic peoples came to be in Gaul. In Gaul it is easy to discern ongoing Etruscan, Greek, and Roman influences on southern Celts living in places like the Rhone Valley, in such things as pottery, trade in wine, adoption of a Latin alphabet for some funerary inscriptions, use of iron currency bars, development of coinages, and an increasing emphasis on agriculture as opposed to stock-rearing. Celts who had settled in Cis-Alpine Gaul were even writing in Latin by the first century B.C. Within Britain, only the southeast of England had come to share to any significant extent in some of these advances by the time of the Roman invasion.

Ireland was the least affected and remained the home of primitive tribal cultures with wealth still traditionally denominated in cattle. To the two major Irish Celtic stock festivals of Beltane on 1st May (putting of animals out to graze) and Samhain on 1st November (autumn slaughter of fatstock), plus the minor festival of Imbolc on 1st February (lambing), did come to be added the later agrarian festival of Lugnasad on 1st August (beginning of harvesting), ascribed in mythology to a late-coming group of settlers.

Although thus diverse, the Celts were clearly distinct from Romans, Etruscans, and Greeks to the south, and from Germanic peoples such as the Franks, Goths, Angles, Saxons, Frisians, Jutes, Norse, and Danes that came to inhabit lands to the east. The Celts were the ancestors of the British peoples – "ancient Britons" in fact.

Some authorities argue plausibly for a significant

5

pre-Celtic element in the British population, but hard evidence is understandably scanty and, in any event, by the time of our story it is the Celtic peoples who are our main concern. The extinct language of the Picts, however, from what little can be deduced about it, seems to comprise both Celtic and archaic non-Celtic elements. The Picts were themselves incorporated by the Irish (Scots) of Dalraida in the 9th century (hence the name Scotland) and, in any event, only play a peripheral role in our story.

Linguistically, what have descended as Celtic languages comprise two branches: the Goidelic languages of Irish, Gaelic, and Manx; and the Brythonic languages of Welsh, Breton, and Cornish. These names give an accurate representation of the areas to which the Celts had been reduced by successive barbarian invasions by the time of the Age of Saints. The present situation is that Cornish and Manx are irreversibly dead. The last native Cornish speaker died in the 1840s and the last native Manx speaker died in the mid 1970s. Gaelic and Irish are not now widely spoken, although Irish enjoys a (controversial) measure of state support in Eire. Breton (700,000 native speakers representing about half of the population of Brittany) survives, but is under constant threat from an unsympathetic central government in Paris. Welsh (600,000 native speakers) enjoys a measure of state support, for example a television service, although it is spoken by only a minority (20%) of the Welsh population today.

This frail Celtic Fringe of western Europe, this precious relic of our roots and the setting of our story, is thus capable of ethnographic, geographical, cultural, and linguistic definition. Furthermore, and very significantly, it was linked by the sea.

The sea was not a barrier to communication but a highway. With prevailing winds between southwest and northwest, seagoing currachs with the wind on their quarter could readily cross the Bay of Biscay, the English and Bristol Channels, and indeed criss-cross the Irish Sea, now often appropriately called the Celtic Sea. The use of this kind of boat of hides stretched over a skeletal wooden framework persisted through millennia up to the early 20th century in the remote Aran Islands off western Ireland. Distances were not enormous. For example, the hills of Ireland, Galloway, northern England, and North Wales can all be easily seen from Man, and no more than twelve miles separates the Antrim coast from the Mull of Kintyre. With due attention to strong tidal currents the Minch and its inside passages could be navigated to the Hebrides and beyond. These voyages, of course, were not without their inherent dangers, not to mention the spread of epidemics of ship-borne plague that reached Wales and Ireland in c.547 and 664.

Although very few members of the Celtic Church have ever been formally canonised by Rome, and most will lie forever unsung, a significant number are remembered by Celtic peoples as Saints. Tangible remains of the places where these Saints lived and died may be scanty indeed, but certain sites retain to this day a unique aura of sanctity and are increasingly becoming the focus of pilgrimage. Poignantly, the full story of the Age of Saints will never be told as so much is lost for ever. The fragments that have come down to us make, however, for compelling study and meditation. Why should their story be of such importance to us today? I hope that some answers may suggest themselves in the following pages.

First, we must have some appreciation of the physical and historical background to our Age of Saints which had its roots in late Roman Britain and Gaul. From all accounts, the British Isles were highly regarded in Roman times as an attractive and fertile land. In addition to sufficient agricultural produce and livestock to sustain at least an estimated two million inhabitants, Britain yielded valuable resources of minerals including tin, copper, and lead. Exports included these together with hides, wool, and much prized cloth.

No Roman soldier ever set foot in a warlike capacity in Ireland, although we know that there was some trade and contact between Ireland and the Roman fortress-port of Chester and other parts of the west coast of Britain. Agricola himself conversed with an Irish chieftain who visited England. The absence of a Roman presence in Ireland has considerable relevance to our story because, as we shall see, traditional Celtic ways were maintained there until, and indeed after, the advent of Christianity, incidentally in a small population estimated at about 200,000.

Scotland had seen one or two temporary incursions of Roman forces north of the line of the Antonine Wall between the Clyde and Forth. But by the second century the Romans were content to rest further south behind the slightly longer Hadrian's Wall between the Solway and Tyne, and maintain more or less peacable relationships with the British tribes immediately to its north. The inhabitants of Scotland, more particularly those living north of the British and north of the Forth-Clyde line mainly in eastern valleys and coastal plains, were known as Picts. They thus had very little contact with Roman Britain.

By contrast, much of England together with southeast Wales was decisively Romanised. An amazing network of eight thousand miles of truly excellent main roads, supplemented by numerous ports and several important canals, facilitated trade, communications, and administration. These activities came to be centred on important civilian towns that had increasingly taken the place of military camps and fortresses after the occupation. The bulk of the population, development, and prosperity lay in England, particularly concentrated in rich agricultural areas such as the Sussex coast, the North Downs, Somerset, Wiltshire, the Cotswolds extending northeastwards into Northants, and parts of East Anglia. In these areas peace and increasing prosperity remained almost unbroken for many generations. Such items as pottery, tiles, bricks, and mosaic tesserae were obviously in ample supply, and can be found for example in abundance on the sites of towns and some 700 known villas – haciendas on large farming estates. An enormous range of iron tools and implements were manufactured, many of them surprisingly similar in appearance to hand tools in use today. Less likely to be preserved, but substantial, would have been work in leather, wood, wicker, and so

on. From all that we now know, it would seem that life, for example, on a villa let us say near Corinium (Cirencester) in the third and fourth centuries A.D. (when Corinium was the second largest city after London) must have been very pleasant indeed – for its fortunate owners at least.

Western Wales, the West Country, northwestern and northern England, although not intensively settled on a Roman pattern – no villas, for example – were securely under Roman rule as a military zone. Life for the British inhabitants of this military zone presumably continued much as it had done before the Roman occupation. Indeed, in Cornwall and parts of western Wales, the Roman presence was minimal.

The bulk of the population was still British and still spoke Celtic dialects, fairly closely related to Gaulish in France. An increasing minority were educated in Latin, and Latin was the language of trade and the army. Large detachments of the army were recruited overseas and many soldiers accepted inducements to settle in Britian at the end of their service, notably in and around the four coloniae of Colchester, Gloucester, Lincoln, and York. No doubt some kind of pigeon-Latin was widely understood in the country at large. Many, if not most, of the wealthy landed families would have been British, and British people would have come to fill many administrative posts. An analogy that is never far from one's mind is the one that could be made with India, perhaps also with British colonial Africa, in the decades leading up to independence (making the substitution, of course, of ancient Briton for native Indian or African, and bearing in mind also the much longer duration of the colonial Roman presence in Britain).

Although on the fringe of Roman Europe, this fair and prosperous land of Britian was well protected and reasonably secure. Hadrian's Wall, the largest military work of the Roman Empire, kept the Picts and other northern tribes at bay and was garrisoned until the end of the 4th century. Strong forts with vessels and quick-response cavalry based at Lancaster, Ribchester, Chester, Segontium (Caernarvon), and Caer Gybi (Holyhead) were sufficient to curtail any tendency of the Irish to deviate from trading to marauding. The eleven imposing forts of the "Saxon Shore" extending from East Anglia to Kent, Sussex, and Hampshire, built mainly towards the end of the 3rd century, performed a similar function against threatened incursions from Saxons and others. And we know of many lesser forts, signal stations, etc. on the also vulnerable Yorkshire, Cumberland, and Welsh coasts and elsewhere. Cavalry and foot soldiers in places like Colchester and London, and in the three great legionary fortresses of York, Chester, and Caerleon (probably the most imposing of their kind anywhere in the Empire) provided an adequate strategic reserve, all operating within an inferable central command structure on this, the Roman Empire's own "North-West Frontier". It is known, for example, that total standing armed forces in Britain at the beginning of the third century were about 50,000 – a very considerable commitment indeed for the times. To pursue the analogy mentioned above, it is interesting to recall that the numerically largest standing army in the world in 1939 was the Indian, much of it having seen active service on rotation on the North-West frontier. In addition to these armed forces, substantial stone walls silently stood guard around some forty towns in Roman England.

A man, his sons, and grandsons, and their grandsons too, could indeed have lived their entire lives in peace and security in many parts of Roman Britain. There were, however, some ominous rumblings, possibly more obvious to us now with the wisdom of hindsight than to the inhabitants of the time. It should be borne in mind that Roman Britain was geographically remote from the centre of the Empire. And for purposes of civil administration, prosperous and prized though it may have been, Britian was merely an outlying diocese and for a long period subordinate to a prefect of Gaul based at Trier.

Trouble for Britain was in fact to develop from both within and without. A pattern for future events had been set as early as 196 when governor Clodius Albinus removed troops from Britain to support his abortive bid for the imperial throne. In their absence,

Hadrian's Wall and York were overrun from the north, but the situation was promptly restored in 197 by Virius Lupus.

The increasing instability of the late Roman Empire is shown, for example, by Allectus usurping authority in Britain during the years 293 to 296 after assassinating Carausius, himself a usurper. This time it took three years for Rome to collect a force to suppress Allectus.

Annoying seaborne Saxon raids commenced at the beginning of the 3rd century. Later that same century, the Picts became increasingly sophisticated seagoing raiders, thus bypassing Hadrian's Wall. They had to be stayed by a large Roman fleet based and victualled at Arbeia (South Shields). And, before the century was out, Irish had started to raid the western coasts of mainland Britain. These seaborne raids all had the potential to become serious, as so much of prosperous Britain was vulnerable, lying near to coasts or to major navigable rivers.

But help generally came from Rome via Gaul. The Emperor Constantius himself was in personal command of military forces in northern England when he died at York in 306. His son Constantine the Great was proclaimed Emperor there in that same year. The Emperor Constans was the last to fight personally in England (342–3). Julian sent forces in 360. Nevertheless, there ensued a serious invasion by a conjunction of Irish, Pictish and Saxon raiders in 367. On this occasion, Emperor Valentian promptly sent Theodosius with reinforcements to restore the situation, which he did after two years hard fighting.

But if help arrived via Gaul, Gaul was also the route

to Rome. Magnus Maximus (Macsen of the Mabinogion), governor of Britain, denuded the island of many troops when he set off in 383 with pretensions to the Emperorship on his ill-fated sortie to Gaul, where he set up his court at Trier. In 387 he advanced into Italy where he was defeated by Emperor Theodosius I and executed at Aquileia in 388. This episode brought to an end the Roman military presence in much of western Wales permanently, and had the effect of greatly accelerating Irish immigration there.

Nevertheless, the *Notitia Dignitatum*, drawn up mainly in 393, records still powerful standing armed forces in Britain. The last record of reinforcements from Rome is of those sent by commander-in-chief Stilicho (himself, incidentally, the son of a Vandal chieftain) in the last five years of the 4th century.

But by now the writing was certainly on the wall. In 406–7 no fewer than three usurpers set themselves up at the head of armed forces in Britain. The first two met sticky ends within a matter of months. The third, a common soldier who called himself Constantine III, took most of the armed forces to Gaul, where on the last day of 406 the Vandals and other invaders from the east had crossed a frontier denuded of troops, a crossing facilitated by a frozen Rhine. Determined Saxon invasion of England in 408–9 was met, however, by equally determined resistance from the British.

Then events happened quickly and took an even more decisive turn. The Empire itself had split into two in 395. Rome herself was shortly in dire straits and was sacked by Alaric the Visigoth in 410. In that same year, the Western Emperor Honorius had written (from Ravenna) to the cities of Britain telling them to defend themselves and look to Rome no longer. This may well have been intended as a temporary expedient at the time but, as we know, it was to prove permanent.

What of Christianity in Britain in late Roman time? There is some record of Christian martyrs in England in the second and third centuries, but very little is known of British Christianity in this period. Then, unpredictably, something quite dramatic happened. Following the long-lasting uneasy relationship between Christianity and the Roman State, and after the intense persecution of Christians during the later part of the reign of Diocletian (284–305), perhaps more accurately viewed as a side-effect of an honest attempt to restore the old religion of the Romans, an Edict of Toleration was proclaimed by Galerius in 311. That same year, Constantine the Great was converted to Christianity. The following year, Constantine won his great victory at Milvian Bridge near Rome, his troops fighting under a Christian banner bearing the Chi-Rho symbol. Suddenly, Christianity was adopted as the official religion of the Empire! (although traditional pagan beliefs and practices were not actually proscribed until 392).

The benefit of this to the Christian church was quickly felt in Britain. We know that as early as 314 three bishops representing York, London, and (probably) Lincoln plus two other delegates attended a church council held at Arles in southern France. This, incidentally, would surely seem to argue for the prior existence of some kind of organised Christian church in Britain.

Christian themes figure prominently in 4th-century

artefacts recovered from sites in Britain. Among some well-known examples are the Chi-Rho monogram on silver spoons found at Chedworth villa and on wall paintings at Lutterworth villa. The remarkable central roundel of Christ in a fourth-century mosaic at Hinton St. Mary (now in the British Museum) is one of the first such portraits of Christ known from the Roman Empire.

Some score of similar finds showing an unmistakable Christian influence are known in Britain. Perhaps the most impressive is the hoard of beautiful silverware with Chi-Rho inscriptions, comprising a dish, hanging-lamp bowl, chalice and four cups, found near the Roman town of Durobrivae (just west of Peterborough), and also now in the British Museum. These date to the first half of the fourth century and constitute probably the earliest such collection known from anywhere in Europe. In contrast to these finds mainly from sophisticated villa sites, there is very little indication of Christian sentiment in military sites.

We know that Ninian was able to make the long journey to Rome via Gaul and return to pastoral duties in Galloway and to missionary activity among the Britons of Strathclyde and, reputedly, among the Picts, in the late 4th century. His base was a modest but famous whitewashed stone-built chapel, the Casa Candida (literally, "the white house") at Whithorn in Galloway, founded in 397. What may just conceivably be a fragment of the original foundations is visible there today. We also know that a well-educated British Christian called Pelagius travelled from Britain to Rome in 380 and on to Africa and Asia Minor. We shall refer to him later.

So we have convincing evidence therefore in late Roman times of some degree of adoption of Christianity by the British (but no reliable indication at all of the actual proportion of Christians in the population at large), a nascent church organisation, and a freedom and facility of travel enjoyed by Christians and, of course, others between Britain and the continent.

III   THE DARK AGES

When Roman authority and assistance were withdrawn (as it proved, for ever) from Britain in 410, there was no sudden collapse of civilisation. We know that the offices of local governers and magistrates with Latin names and titles persisted. Schools continued. A British variety of Latin remained in widespread use. "Romano-British" civic life in many major towns thus continued, despite some inferable reduction in economic activity and trade and the cessation of minting of new coins early in the fifth century. Indeed, archaeological evidence has been interpreted to indicate significant new building in Uriconium (the capital town of the Cornovii, near Shrewsbury) during the century after 450. Even as late as 540, the inscription on a memorial stone in remote Penmachno, Gwynedd, apparently refers to the Consul Justinian.

We also know that a Christian church continued, and probably even grew. Fairly numerous place names including the word Eccles or its derivatives attest Christian centres of this period. Continuity in both ecclesiastical and secular matters is demonstrated, for example, by the family of St. Patrick, a native of western Britain, born possibly near the Solway Firth, and who died in the second half of the fifth century (the precise year is hotly disputed). His grandfather Potitus had been a priest, and his father Calpornius a deacon. Calpornius was also a decurion (town councillor) and was the fortunate owner of a country estate.

More than likely, some reasonable degree of law and order was maintained in London, the seat of the diocese of Britain, within the four coloniae mentioned above, and also within the thirty or so "civitates", each a local government area, often tribally defined, and with an important town as its centre. In all probability, too, effective local militias could be raised by these.

What was fatally different, however, was the apparent collapse of a centralised civil service and tax-gathering, and the consequent lack of a sufficiently powerful armed force under centralised command – indeed the lack of any powerful central authority in the vacuum left by the withdrawal of Rome. This potential lack of any base for concerted action courted disaster by reason of the ever-present threat of invasion by others jealous of Britain's considerable prosperity.

Britain was, in fact, slowly but perceptibly reverting to tribal societies, reminiscent in some ways of the time of the Roman invasion four centuries previously. There is convincing evidence, for example, that some hill forts, such as the Romans had found and conquered, were reoccupied and reinforced in the 5th and 6th centuries. Commerce and prosperity declined, as shown for example by the replacement of sophisticated pottery, once traded over considerable distances, by crude locally produced domestic pottery. One could make an analogy with the sad contemporary history of some of post-colonial Africa.

Tradition has it that the final debacle began around

the middle of the 5th century when Vortigern (a prominent figure – but not a *national* leader?) invited three
shiploads of Saxon mercenaries under Hengist and
Horsa to southeast England in order to bolster defence
against raiding Pictish invaders from the north. The
result, we are not surprised to be told, was rather like
inviting foxes inside the chicken-house in order to provide for its protection. The mercenaries became
invaders and settlers themselves. Vortigern, we are
told, disgraced and disconsolate, fled westwards to a fort
called Dinas Emrys near Beddgelert and later to Tre'r
Ceiri, a remarkably well-preserved stone-built hill fort
in a remote part of the Lleyn Peninsula, where he died.

But the truth, although not known in detail, is certainly more complex than this tale might suggest.

One has to say that some history books (and a recent
TV documentary series) about the English tend to give
an impression of noble and intrepid warriors and
explorers venturing bravely by boat to Kent, East
Anglia, Selsey Bill, or up the Solent to settle and found
this wonderful nation of ours, and make little or no
mention of the British – rather like equally prevalent
histories of America starting with Columbus and other
European explorers and settlers!

The facts lend themselves to a different emphasis.
What actually crossed the Channel were uncouth, illiterate, belligerent, pagan savages. They had not been
subject to civilising influences such as had the Goths.
They were, quite literally, the scum of Europe. Indications are that, to some significant extent, they followed
policies not unlike those which we have had to wait
until the last decade of our glorious 20th century to
coin a term for, namely, "ethnic cleansing" in the fair

land they invaded of its civilised inhabitants, the British.

The invaders did not come in overwhelming numbers and initially, as mentioned above, resistance by the British around the years 408 and 409 had been determined and successful. But gradually a veil of darkness descended over Britain from the east. It is perhaps just as well that we do not have accurate records of its ongoing horrors. Doubtless there were reverses to both sides and there were periods of relative calm. Probably, for the most part it was a question of slow infiltration by the invaders and westward flight of the British, coupled with localised uncouth squabbles over land. Neither of the two races had anything in the nature of centralised government and there are no reliable historical records. In this period of increasing anarchy, change may even have appeared to be slow to many of the more fortunate native British living away from actual contact with the invaders. In 429 a bloodless British victory over some of the invaders was achieved somewhere in the Midlands in the presence of Bishop Germanus. Germanus, the leading churchman of Gaul, had come over from Auxerre (situated on the River Yonne some 100 miles southeast of Paris) on the first of two visits to combat the Pelagian heresy, of which more anon. Apparently, he took the odd battle (or was it just a skirmish?) against the barbarians in his stride. The barbarian English are reputed to have fled when Germanus raised the cry of Hallelujah. This episode would seem to have started the tradition, now more than fifteen centuries old, that the Christian God is always on the side of the British in their numerous wars!

But the beachheads established by:

Jutes, coming from northern Denmark (Jutland), in Kent, Isle of Wight, and Hampshire, and in Kent perhaps including a few relatively civilised Franks coming from northeast Gaul,

Angles, coming from southern Denmark, in Northumbria and East Anglia,

Saxons, coming from northwest Germany, in Essex, Sussex, and Wessex (the East, South, and West Saxons respectively), and

Frisians, coming from the eastern Netherlands coast, in Lincolnshire, inexorably grew and coalesced into major settlements. Let us refer to these barbarians here jointly as English. Much later, from the time of Alfred's successful fight back against the Danes, it was, of course, the (now civilised) Saxons who had become predominant amongst the English.

Out of the mists of history comes a record of one Briton, Ambrosius Aurelius, achieving victories, possibly in Wiltshire, that stemmed the tide of barbarian advance, at least temporarily, at some time in the mid 5th century. Gildas records a number of British victories over the English in the early 6th century, the most decisive being the last at Badon in c.518. Later writers have associated King Arthur with these battles. The North Country, the West Country, Wiltshire, the Welsh Border, have all competed for the honour of being the setting for the victories of Arthur. There may well in fact have been a successful chieftain of that name at this time, but a "king", no – the sad truth was that Britain was no longer a kingdom.

The English advance proved to be relentless. After an apparent lull in the first half of the sixth century, decisive major battles were fought by the West Saxons at Old Sarum in 552, Barbury Castle near Swindon in 556, and at Dyrham near Bath in 577. These battles won Wiltshire and Gloucestershire for the invaders, thus driving a permanent division by land between the British of the Cornish peninsula and those further north. Another bloody battle near Chester in 615, including the massacre by the Northumbrian Angles of numerous British monks of Bangor-on-Dee (who had been imprudent enough to cheer on the British fighters from the sidelines), further divided the British of Wales from those in Cumbria and Strathclyde, at least temporarily. Much of the north of England was to remain a battleground for another generation.

The eventual victory of the English was sweeping, as evidenced by the virtual obliteration of British languages in the occupied areas, where only a few Celtic names, mainly of major rivers and of other natural features such as large areas of uncleared woodland, tend to survive. A complete trawl for words of possible British origin in Anglo-Saxon has produced about a dozen only. Interestingly, and by contrast, following the Norman invasion five centuries later, the language of the conquered eventually prevailed over that of the conquerors.

There indeed ensued an enormous break with the Roman past in the overrun areas. Latin was lost, towns were abandoned, villa sites were generally no longer inhabited, and all forms of government collapsed. Nothing was heard even of London for nearly one and a half centuries after 457. The fine Roman roads remained, only to serve as convenient highways for further armed excursions by the invaders. Some came to be barricaded by massive earthern dykes.

We have only one first-hand account of the eventual fate of the Britons in the overrun areas, that by the monk Gildas (in his infuriating flowery style, long on rhetoric and short on facts), written in the middle of the sixth century:

There was no burial to be had except in the ruins of houses or in the bellies of beasts and birds. . . . A number of the wretched survivors were caught in the mountains and butchered wholesale. Others, their spirit broken by hunger, went to surrender to the enemy; they were fated to be slaves for ever, if indeed they were not killed straight away, the highest boon. Others made for lands beyond the sea. Others held out, though not without fear, in their own land, trusting their lives with constant foreboding to the high hills, steep, menacing, and fortified, to the densest forests, and to the cliffs of the sea coast.

The tone parallels the concise and much earlier *Groans of the British* addressed to the Roman ruler Aetius in Gaul in c.446:

> The barbarians drive us into the sea, the sea drives us back to the barbarians. Between these two means of death we are either killed or drowned.

One poignant episode is recorded in the great bardic classic, *The Gododdin*, composed in northern dialect Brittonic (similar to Welsh at that time) and attributed to the poet Aneirin. Only poems attributed to Taliesin are older. It begins thus, in true bardic fashion: "This is the Gododdin; Aneirin sang it". It records the despairing and disastrous last battle of a three-hundred strong band of British warriors who rode bravely south from Edinburgh in c.590 to confront the Northumbrian Angles. Aneirin tells us that the warriors were gentle and sage in civilian life, but fearless and terrible in battle. Only three returned. Aneirin pays this last tribute to their dead:

> They had earned their mead, but became food for ravens. . . . Though they were slain they slew, and they shall be honoured until the end of the world.

Speaking from the English side, Bede gives this rather clinical account of a comparable battle fought in 603:

> Alarmed at his [the Northumbrian Ethelfrid's] advance, Aidan, King of those Scots [Irish who lived in Britain], came against him with a large and

strong army, but was defeated and fled with very few, having lost almost his entire army at a place known as Degsastan.... From that day until the present, no king of the Scots in Britain has dared to do battle with the English.

A contemporary analogy could well be drawn with countries like Mozambique and Somalia, where our TV screens have shown how anarchy, rapine, crop-failure, famine and disease have the potential to quickly decimate by death or flight a native population that is utterly dependent on its livestock and on crops for food and for next year's seed on a year to year basis. Fifth- and 6th-century Britain no longer, of course, enjoyed anything at all in the nature of international aid. And Britain was not alone in this experience. The whole of the Roman Empire in western Europe had dissolved into Germanic realms, although nowhere with such catastrophic and anarchic results as in England. Another thought-provoking contemporary analogy might be with the ongoing experience of the Palestinians at the hands of the Israelis who first arrived in force by boat in the late 1940s at the time of the end of the British mandate. Savage retribution by determined invaders might well have followed any pathetic isolated acts of resistance by the native population. And in the same general context of invaders and settlers we should also not forget the pushing back and decimation of the native populations of the Americas and Australia by invading adventurers and settlers mainly of European Christian stock.

After several generations of inferable horror, by the end of the 7th century the tide of English advance, now increasingly well-documented from the archaeological study of their burial sites, was stemmed uneasily more or less at the boundaries of Cornwall, Wales, Cumbria (land of the Cymry = Welsh = Britons), and Strathclyde. In the meantime, there had been a considerable migration of British people into Brittany, peaking in the late 5th and mid 6th centuries. Brittany owes its name to this exodus of Britons.

The areas into which the British had been pushed were in general hilly, wetter, and less productive agriculturally than much of England. Accordingly, the population they could support and the affluence they could generate were small. It has been estimated that by the end of the 7th century the total population of England and Wales was around 600,000 of which, significantly, less than half would have been British. This (very rough) estimate should be compared with estimates of at least two million British inhabitants by late Roman times.

The Christian church was also in retreat from the invaders, although there is, here and there, some scant evidence of continuity. It is possible, indeed probable, that enclaves of British, some of them Christian, survived the wave of English advance. For example, my native Wallasey, then virtually an island separated from Wirral by tidal marshes, derives its name from Walea, literally "Welsh island", i.e., a Germanic name recognising the contemporary existence of Britons. Once invaders become settlers, they have something to lose as well as to gain by rapine, and, despite the overall general advance of the English, local accommodations may have been reached with some native British. For example, admittedly much later than the times of the initial barbarous invasions, indigenous Britons were given an acknowledged place in West Saxon society as recorded in the Laws of Ine promulgated in 690. The Britons living there with the Saxons were not necessarily slaves; some were free men. The survival of "Eccles" place names, mentioned above, is thought to attest continuing British church settlements. There is a concentration of these names in Lancashire, Derbyshire, and Cheshire (i.e., places where the English arrived late), but also two on the Stratford Avon and another two in East Anglia. Mailos (Old Melrose) and Abercurnig (Abercorn, west of Edinburgh) are examples of possible British Christian foundations surviving the maelstrom. When the (by then Christian) Northumbrian Angles arrived at Whithorn in far western Galloway in the early 8th century, they found Irish monks there continuing to work on the humble site where Ninian had worked four centuries previously (the site affords nearby safe landfalls in any wind and a short sea crossing to Ireland). The Northumbrian bishop Pechthelm, a friend of Bede's, took over there in c.730. But Northumbrian Angles had previously sacked Whithorn in the late sixth century and had burned the precious library of Candida Casa.

We should not rely on these relatively isolated instances to conclude that there was any nation-wide continuance of an organised Christian church in the areas that were being overrun by the barbarians. Far from it. In particular, there is no evidence at all to suggest that any invading barbarians were locally converted to Christianity by indigenous Britons. On the contrary, the latter more than likely entertained the unchristian thought that the pagan barbarians thoroughly merited eternal damnation!

In the midst of all this strife and uncertainty, we know of an uncomfortable and inconclusive meeting between Augustine of Canterbury (whom we will meet again later) and seven British bishops in 604. Various suggested sites for this meeting include Chester, Abberley, Cressage, Cricklade, and Aust-on-Severn, i.e. all lying at or near the boundary of English advance at the time. This was undoubtedly an honest initiative by Augustine to reconcile the two churches, the Roman and the Celtic, with a view to organising Christianity countrywide in Britain. It was regarded, however, by the British bishops more as an attempt to impose foreign dictatorship. It is said that Augustine sat under an oak and did not rise to meet them as equals but remained seated as if to accept their obeisance. The failed outcome of this meeting set the seal on the separate development of the Celtic church in its lonely western outposts for at least another two generations.

This, then, is a brief outline of the unpromising physical and social background to our improbable but true story of the Celtic church and its Saints. In contrast to the isolation of the Celtic church, it is interesting to note that the Goths who sacked Rome had already been converted in large numbers to Christianity in the late fourth century. This ensured a continuity of the Christian tradition in Italy, as also in Spain and Yugoslavia. In France too, Clovis, the powerful king of the invading Franks (a Germanic tribe) based in north-eastern France, was converted to Roman Christianity and baptized in Reims on Christmas Day 496. Clovis was apparently content to leave much of the rest of

Gaul in the hands of a Gallo-Roman aristocracy and church organisation, again resulting in a continuity of church tradition.

Among the earliest Christian figures known to us from the Age of Saints is Dubricius, Dyfrig in Welsh. He is in fact one of the few to be more commonly known by his Latin name. He was born near Madley in Hereford-shire around the year 450 and ministered in the sur-rounding district of Archenfield, centred on the Wye around Hereford between Ross and Hay. He founded a church at Hentland (the name looks English but is cor-rupted from Henllan in Welsh, meaning simply "old church settlement") some eight miles south of Here-ford down the River Wye, and another at Moccas (another Welsh name, Moch Rhos, meaning "moor of the swine"), ten miles west of Hereford up-river. This area, an agriculturally rich one, which contains four other churches dedicated to Dubricius, lay far enough west and inland to escape early overrunning by bar-barian English invaders. There is no mention of Dubri-cius ever having been a monk, although in later life he enjoyed passing Lents with monks on the island of Caldey, and he retired to the monastic settlement on Bardsey Island where he died c.522. Moreover, he is invariably referred to as father or bishop. Dubricius, then, would seem to represent a carry-over of the pas-toral Christian church in a part of Romano-British

Britain enjoying some degree of prosperity and continuity of Christian tradition well into the sixth century.

Foundations of a small church inside the Roman fort at Caerwent and Christian burials on the site of a Roman villa at Llantwit Major, some thirty miles to the west, may also date from this early period. Caerwent, alias Venta Silurum, was the tribal capital of the Silures, along with the Cornovii based on Uriconium (near Shrewsbury) the only Romanised Welsh, and probably the first Christians in Wales.

Then, alas, we can only assume disintegration of ecclesiastical organisation and bishoprics. We see no more Dyfrigs. Instead, what eventually took their place was a kind of monasticism, which by this time had already become a powerful and growing movement in Gaul.

Monastic Christianity originated in Egypt and other parts of the Near East. Almost from its beginnings, one can discern three strands in the monastic movement.

The first is an austere, solitary, hermit-like withdrawal from the world with its distractions and temptations, traditionally to the "desert", where an individual can live alone in piety and peace, have time to meditate, and find communion with God – perhaps a rather self-centred and unproductive saintliness?

The second, which came a little later, involved living in some degree of solitude but banded together in a community and worshipping God, all living according to some strict rule. This kind of monastic life offered the real possibility of forming a centre for preserving, extending, and transmitting a scholarly tradition of learning. The first true monastery in this sense was that of Pachomius, who was born in Egypt c.290 and who died at the monastery, which he had founded, of Tabennisi on the Nile in central Egypt in 346. He was actually preceded by Antony, born near Memphis in c.251 and who died at a very ripe old age in 356. Antony had gathered hermitical monks into loosely knit communities and exercised some leadership over them, visiting them occasionally, but remained himself a much-respected solitary for most of his time – his communities were a sort of transition stage to what we might now regard as normal monastic life. Somewhat later than both Antony and Pachomius was Basil, c.330–79, whose rule still forms the basis of monastic life in the Orthodox church.

The third and last is a similar organised monastic community, but devoted in part to travelling, missionary work, and founding new communities, the so-called "peregrini", a mission typified also by some Friars of later medieval times.

The Celtic church was to strongly embrace the monastic tradition and was to encompass all the above three possibilities in good measure. It was the second that was to have a greater lasting influence than the first, understandably so. And it was the third that, eventually, coupled with the second, was to have the greatest influence of all.

Looking now nearer to our shores, monasticism reputedly came to Gaul with Martin of Tours (c.315–97), who founded the monastery of Ligugé, some five miles south of Poitiers, in 360. In 371, Martin was consecrated bishop of Tours, a pleasant Gallo-Roman town in the Loire valley, but his main interest seems to have been a monastery which he founded at nearby Marmoutier. This monastery attracted many visitors, among them Elen, wife of the above-mentioned Magnus Maximus, and almost certainly Ninian. The tradition that Illtud (see below) studied at Marmoutier is plausible but not certain. Ligugé and Marmoutier were joined by many other monasteries in Gaul, a total of about sixty at the beginning of the 6th century and about two hundred at its end. Marmoutier was eventually overtaken in importance by one founded by Honoratus in 410 on the island of Lérins offshore from Cannes. It is fair to say that Lérins and Marmoutier remained pre-eminent among all the Gaulish monasteries in preserving a wide cultural and teaching tradition.

Contact with these Gaulish monasteries led to the first British monasteries. As mentioned above, we are aware of an early and ongoing Christian (and monastic?) tradition at Whithorn in Galloway, following in the footspeps of Ninian. Archaeological evidence now indicates that Tintagel may well lay claim to being the site of the first true British monastery, perhaps rivalled in antiquity by early monastic settlements near Lismore in the Blackwater valley of southeastern Ireland. But it seems that it is to Wales we now have to look in large measure for our story of the monastic evolution of the Celtic church.

There is a strong tradition, supported by several dedications, that (monastic?) Christian settlements were founded by the sons of Elen, perhaps even by Elen herself, on her return to Wales from France and contact with Martin of Tours, following the defeat and execution of her ambitious husband Magnus Maximus in 388. The sons in question are Peblig (Latin Publicus) and Cystennin (Latin Constantine). Their names are indeed recorded in the churches of Llanpeblig adjacent to the Roman fort at Segontium (Caernarvon) and Llangwstenin near Llandudno. If this is true, these would be very early sites, but unfortunately no reliable written confirmation exists. But the name of Elen herself certainly lives on. Many Roman roads in Wales are still known locally as Sarn Helen (Elen's causeway). Coupled with access by sea, they remained important avenues of communication for centuries, and it is a fascinating armchair and field exercise, armed with Ordnance Survey 50,000 maps and Roman Britain map, to study the distribution of ancient Celtic "Llan" sites in relation to Roman roads and other topographic features.

For the first reasonably well-authenticated British monk we look to Illtud, founder of Llanilltud Fawr (the big church settlement of St. Illtud), the name now corrupted to Llantwit Major, in South Wales, some fifteen miles to the west of Cardiff. The date of this important monastic foundation was late 5th century. A reliable, almost contemporary, life of Samson, a famous student of Illtud's, includes the following portrait of Illtud himself:

Now this Eltut was the most learned of all the Britons in his knowledge of all the Scriptures, both the Old Testament and the New Testament and in every branch of philosophy, poetry and rhetoric, grammar and arithmetic.

This, of course, is very much in the humanistic Graeco-Roman tradition of study, with its insistence on literacy and numeracy followed by instruction in philosophy and rhetoric. Illtud is also credited with popularising the use of a new improved kind of plough. All in all, an appealing blend of the scholastic and the practical!

It appears that Illtud (?425–?505; possibly later) came (returned?) to South Wales from Brittany, again illustrative of enduring cross-Channel links. The usual route was actually across the two Channels, Bristol and English, linked by an intervening overland trip across Cornwall. No buildings, illustrated manuscripts, or other artefacts survive from Llanilltud Fawr in the time of Illtud. His fame rests in tradition and in that of the students he personally taught and inspired. These include the above-mentioned Samson, and Aurelius for sure, possibly Gildas, and much less certainly, despite what some hagiographers may have claimed, David, the Patron Saint of Wales. The hagiographers are right, however, in stressing the great influence of Illtud, who appears to us over the centuries as a great and devout man in the noble tradition of a humane and educated "Roman" Christian, albeit a Celt.

In part contemporary with Illtud was another very famous saint, Cadog. Cadog, we are told, was a native Briton from South Wales, son of Glywys, an early ruler in Glamorgan. The monastery Cadog founded at Llan-carfan, just six miles to the east of Llanilltud Fawr, also now vanished without trace, came to enjoy comparable fame to Illtud's for its teaching excellence. A strong tradition claims that the greatest of all early Irish monks, Finnian of Clonard, was trained by Cadog. If true, this was indeed a major seminal event in the history of the Celtic church, as we will appreciate later when we consider the Celtic church in Ireland.

So we have these two monasteries, close together, preserving a Romano-British tradition and some degree of classical scholarship, precariously sandwiched between barbarians to the east and wild Welsh and immigrant Irish to the west. Their high repute continued throughout their long history up to Norman times. Interestingly, their sites, close to both the coast and the major Roman east–west road in lowland South Wales, seem to welcome communication. They both lie within a few miles of the important hillfort citadel of Dinas Powys, which is known to have been occupied and receiving imports from the Mediterranean in the 6th century.

In contrast to these eminent "scholastic" monastic foundations, we know of several monastic "retreats", often on relatively inaccessible sites. One early one is Caldey, just offshore from Tenby, founded early in the 6th century. Mention must also be made of the fabulous isle of Bardsey, founded by Cadfan also in the early 6th century. Bardsey lies a bare two or three miles off the tip of the Lleyn Peninsula in northwest Wales, but between the island and the main is a most dangerous tide race. The modern Welsh name is Ynys Enlli, the island of tides. Many monks took refuge on Bardsey after the bloody massacre at Bangor-on-Dee mentioned above. Bardsey was reckoned to be a healthy spot. The monks were reputed to live long and die peacefully in order of age, a noteworthy phenomenon in an era when all were well acquainted with the Reaper's work. Another island retreat was Grassholm in the middle of the Bristol Channel, where Gildas lived for a while. The existence of these sites reinforces our impression of the considerable proficiency in seamanship of the times.

We should now refer to an unexpected twist in our story – the Irish connection. Perhaps we should not be too surprised. The Mabinogion, although composed of imagery and legends, cannot be entirely devoid of fact and is, of course, full of stories linking Wales, Ireland, Cornwall and Brittany. And we have already mentioned the great extent of Irish immigration into western Wales (plus Cornwall), an immigration which probably peaked in the fifth century. Some of the later Irish immigrants may already have been Christian. For example, tradition relates the story of Tathan, the son of an Irish King, who sailed to the mouth of the Severn and was granted land there to build a church. One important, distinguished, and better documented line of descent comes through Brychan. Brychan was the son of Marchel, herself the daughter of the Welsh King Tewdrig who died fighting the English at a place not far from Tintern. Marchel had traveled in state to Ireland to marry Prince Anlach, the son of King Coromac. They returned together to Wales and settled in the district of Brecon (the name is derived from Brychan). Later hagiography has ascribed to Brychan an enormous progeny, many of them Christian saints with numerous dedications in southern Wales.

What is interesting in this, furthermore, is the implicit acknowledgment of settling by Irish and intermarriage between them and the British. The Irish spoke a comparable language and, although invasive, they would never have been loathed by the British with anything like the same intensity as they loathed the English. From the point of view of the Irish, the British were civilised and literate, and thus clearly had something to offer. Numerous memorial stones, main-

ly in southwest Wales, coupled with a few in northwest
Wales, speak to us with the names of deceased Irish-
men written in Ogham and Latin (as opposed to solely
in Ogham in Ireland itself). One from Eglwys Gymyn
just north of Pendine records Avitoria, grand-daughter
or great-grand-daughter of Brychan himself.

This silent testimony of the stones thus witnesses a
most important development: the contact of a vigorous
and unromanised Ireland, still living in the Iron Age,
with literate British (and Gaulish) monastic Christianity. As we shall see, this union was to prove
immensely fertile and to have far-reaching results.

Let us return to consider some of the pupils of Illtud.
Of these, the most illustrious was certainly Samson.
Born some time between 480 and 486, he was taken by
his parents at the age of five to study at Llanilltud. Of
course, the only possible place where a bright child of
that time could receive an education was at a
monastery. He progressed rapidly and was ordained as
deacon at Llanilltud in the first decade of the 6th century by none other than Dyfrig. He spent some time on
Caldey Island where, after its first abbot Piro had died
after falling drunk down the well, he became abbot.
During his abbacy, he took the opportunity to visit Ireland in company with some learned Irish who had
stopped over at Caldey on their long journey back from
Rome through Gaul. Samson went on to spend some
time in Cornwall, where he received hospitality from
Petroc at Padstow and from Dochau at St. Kew, both on
or near the estuary of the River Camel. Then, after a
short overland journey, Samson sailed from the Fowey
to Brittany where, after some time, he founded the
prestigious monastery of Dol, which eventually

became Brittany's foremost religious centre. Recognised as the most eminent churchman in Brittany, Samson visited Paris where he was successful in obtaining the release of a Breton Prince. He took part in another visit to Paris in 557 for a church council concerned, inter alia, with the organisation of the Breton church. Samson died peacefully on 28th July 560 at Dol and was buried there. Pilgrims came to visit his sarcophagus there for many centuries. Later, even the Saxon kings Edward the Elder and Aethelstan were to hold him in high esteem.

The details of Samson's life are recorded in the above-mentioned biography written around 610–15 by a monk of Dol who included notes and information supplied to him by an octagenarian nephew of Samson's cousin Henoc. The life has a few implausible miracles thrown in for good measure, but is nevertheless convincingly authentic in a broad historical context. It is easily the earliest biography of a British Celtic Saint. It helped set the pattern for the considerable number of Saint's Lives that were to be penned in the succeeding centuries – with varying degrees of respect for the hard facts!

Another of Illtud's pupils was Aurelius (also known as Paul Aurelian and, in Welsh, Peulin) whose life was completed in 884 by the monk Wrmonoc of Landevennec in Brittany. Although penned rather a long time after the death of Aurelius, this life (itself claimed to be based on an earlier, now vanished, manuscript) also ranks as an important ancient primary source. In spite of being replete with some legendary and doubtful material, the life does convincingly describe how Aurelius was the son of a Welsh chieftain and came to be educated at the monastery of Illtud. Like Samson, he also migrated to Brittany via Cornwall. The ancient church of Paul near Penzance is one of several dedications to him there. After founding a number of churches in Brittany he became bishop at the place now called after him, Saint-Pol-de-Leon, and died in old age at his monastery on the nearby island of Batz.

It is interesting to note how the surviving patterns of ancient church dedications tie in very well with the documented accounts of these saints' doings. It is not unreasonable therefore to look to similar patterns in order to lend some confirmation to events described in suspect lives of other saints written after even greater intervals of time after their deaths. Note again the ongoing close links between Wales, Cornwall, and Brittany.

The monk Gildas (?500–?570) who, as mentioned above, has given us our only contemporary account of historical events in early 6th-century Britain, may also have been a student at Llanilltud. He was a man who commanded a wide Latin vocabulary and could quote some Latin classics with ease. According to Breton tradition, in 555 Gildas also went to Brittany, founded the monastery at Rhuys, and died on the island of Houat about 570.

Saint Padarn is said to have had links with both Illtud and Cadog. He founded a monastery at Llanbadarn Fawr just inland from Aberystwyth, which, although not quite of the stature of Llanilltud Fawr or Llancarfan, maintained a reputation as a centre of learning for several centuries.

In strong contrast to the above-mentioned saints of a Romano-British classical mould, we have two saints,

Teilo and David (Dewi in Welsh), linked together by tradition and by numerous dedications in southwest Wales. They founded monastic settlements at Llandeilo and St. David's, the latter also known as Mynyw or Menevia, respectively. Surprisingly, considering that David is the Patron Saint of Wales, not much is known of either of them in detail. The earliest surviving life of David, in fact, is one written by Rhygyfarch at Llanbadarn Fawr in c.1190. David and Teilo were products of the wild west of Wales, quite dissimilar to the more urbane and scholarly Illtud and associates. David, particularly, comes across as a simple and uncompromising evangelist and bible-thumper. His nickname, it is said, was "the Waterman", alluding to his temperance, in an age when ale was considered (quite properly) good food. David reputedly died on 1st March 589 but the precise date, although of course observed in Wales, is probably unreliable.

Further north along the Welsh coast, we are aware of an early saint, Sadwrn, from an early type of Latin epitaph to him dated c.530 in the ancient church at Llansadwrn in Anglesey. A persistant tradition makes him a brother of Illtud, although more than likely this merely represents the habit of later hagiographers of attempting, unjustifiably, to link saints by kinship.

Somewhat later, we encounter an enigmatic group of saints, known as Letavian, who, judging from dedications, arrived by sea from Pembrokeshire (or even from Brittany?) and founded coastal settlements, sometimes linked to inland ones throughout parts of mid and North Wales. As an example, we can consider Cadfan, whose main settlement was apparently on the coast at Towyn. A memorial stone there commemorates him and his patron Cyngen. The stone itself is written in archaic Welsh and is of uncertain age, but likely represents one of the earliest records of the Welsh language. A few miles inland near Abergynolwen we have "Cadfan's waterfall", "Cadfan's seat", and "Cadfan's track", and just over the hills twenty miles further on to the east we have his ancient settlement of Llangadfan.

In general, it seems that events in North Wales were to take a parallel but separate course to those in the south, some little time later, and with relatively little overlap. We know even less about them in detail. There are some independent historical references but little reliable detailed information. The land is wilder, just that little bit more remote from the more intensively settled areas in Roman times, just a little further from sea links with the continent, and intrinsically, apart perhaps from Anglesey, only capable of sparser settlement.

Tantalising fragments of evidence, for example the Penmachno stones mentioned above, suggest some continuity of Romano-British tradition in local government and Christian church as in southeast Wales. Tradition, place names, types of hut settlements, and Ogham stones, also all attest the immigration of Irish into northwest Wales, just as into southwest Wales.

A landmark in the inferable turbulent history of North Wales is the arrival of Cunedda with a powerful band of followers from Strathclyde at the beginning of the 5th century or possibly even in the late 4th century. Some of them would have been descendants of Ninian's converts in southern Scotland. Tradition declares that after their arrival these British tribesmen drove out most of the Irish immigrants from North Wales. It is just possible that they may even have been deliberately encouraged to resettle in North Wales during the last years of the Roman administration with precisely this end in view. Powerful dynasties, descended from sons of Cunedda, endured for many centuries. Indeed, some of their names persist to the present day, e.g., Gwynedd, Ceredigion, Merioneth. A distinct band of Christian saints operated under their aegis. Many were kin. Hagiographers' tales suggest that relationships between them were sometimes friendly, sometimes strained, sometimes independent, sometimes hilarious.

Two saints, prominent for their work in North Wales, were born in Strathclyde. The first, Deiniol (6th century), is known as "Deiniol of the two Bangors" because he is credited with founding important monasteries at Bangor on the Menai Straits and at Bangor-on-Dee some fifteen miles south of Chester. It was the imprudent monks of this Bangor who were slaughtered by the Northumbrians under Ethelfrith in 615; it is said that the few survivors never stopped running until they had reached Bardsey! Deiniol himself retired and died at Bardsey. At least as well known as Deiniol is another northerner, Kentigern, well known in Scotland by his Celtic nickname Munghu or Mungo. Kentigern (527–600?612) is believed to have founded a church in Glasgow, then to have been engaged in missionary work in Cumbria before coming to North Wales where he established a monastery at Llanelwy (St. Asaph) about 560. He returned to Scotland and was succeeded in c.570 as abbot at Llanelwy by Asaph, whose name is also recorded in the dedication of the nearby ancient church settlement of Llanasa. Asaph and Deiniol were both descendants of the northern chieftain Coel Godebog.

The two most well-known saints of Anglesey are Seiriol and Cybi. Seiriol, a descendant of Cunedda, founded monasteries at Penmon near the southeast tip of the island and on the nearby small island of Ynys Seiriol (also aptly known to Norsemen in times past as Priestholm and to today's English trippers as Puffin Island). Stone remains of a well at Penmon and the outline of a rath and cells on Ynys Seiriol are possible rare tangible remains of actual buildings in use during the Age of Saints. Cybi was apparently of Cornish provenance; two ancient churches are dedicated to him there. Nevertheless, he found his way to Anglesey, where he founded a monastery inside the Roman fort at Holyhead (Caer Gybi). The stone walls of the Roman fort survive, but any possible traces of Cybi's building are presumably overlain by the present-day church, also built inside the fort. Llangybi, in the Lleyn Peninsula, is close to Cybi's ancient well, Ffynnon Cybi, of which some of the stone work may be very ancient.

An engaging little tale links Cybi Felyn, "Cybi the Tawny", with Seiriol Wyn, "Seiriol the Fair". The rationale behind this is that the two saints were friends and were said to be in the habit of playing hookey from their respective monasteries and arranging to meet on certain days at Llanerch-y-medd (the green glade of honey) in the centre of Anglesey. To achieve this, each would have had a walk of twelve miles or so. Cybi, travelling eastward in the morning and returning home westward in the evening, always faced the sun on these excursions, and hence got nicely suntanned. The reverse was the case with Seiriol, who did not have the sun to face and hence retained his monkish pallor. The tale is patently a hagiographer's ridiculous invention, of a type I have attempted to eschew in presenting the evidence. But wait. The two saints, we know, were contemporaries. It is more than likely that they would have had occasion to meet, each picking out his route along a network of narrow walking paths, similar to those linking African villages today, and which at that time would have linked numerous tiny settlements in Anglesey. Is the story then a totally unpardonable invention? Is it not possible that other hagiographers' stories may contain at least a grain of truth?

Dedications to Saint Beuno are nearly as ubiquitous in North Wales as those to David in South Wales. There is no geographical overlap between them. Although Beuno is clearly an important figure and comes rather late in our story, the hard facts about him are surprisingly scarce. He was reputedly born in Shropshire and educated in southeast Wales. He apparently established a church at Llanveynoe (the name is derived from Llan Beuno) near Ewyas in Herefordshire. Then he appears to have moved decisively north to found a monastic settlement at Llanymynech (the settlement of the monks) near Oswestry and was associated with churches at Berriew and Meifod in the same area. A large stone by the side of a lane near Berriew is known to this day locally as Beuno's Stone. Next Beuno turns up in the upper Dee Valley at Gwyddelwern, but eventually he settled in the far northwest of Wales at Clynnog Fawr on the Caernarvonshire coast in north Lleyn, where he died c.630. The church at Clynnog Fawr is built above the foundations of an ancient chapel, and adjacent to a smaller chapel commemorating the saint's tomb and containing a stone with a cross. Clynnog Fawr later became an important gathering point for the great medieval pilgrim routes to Bardsey along the Lleyn Peninsula. To follow them in detail is still an unforgettable experience.

One could go on. But suffice it to say that there are in Wales 614 known ancient Celtic dedications preserving the names of some 300 individual saints. In large measure, these are confined within the present frontier of Wales. In some places, English encroachment, as in western Herefordshire and northwest Salop, has resulted in some Celtic sites now appearing in England. To the north, there is just one name, Landican, remaining in the Wirral peninsula, Cheshire. The name, recording the probable original dedication to Tecwyn, has been corrupted with time, and is also now mispronounced with the accent incorrectly on the first syllable.

Most of the saints' settlements incorporate the word "llan" in their name. This literally means an enclosure, as in Welsh "perllan", an orchard, and refers to the cleared and enclosed plot housing the saint's cell and chapel, which would have been built of traditional materials such as wattle and thatch. The same word reappears frequently in Cornwall and again in the "lons" of Brittany. Early Christian settlements are recorded also by the many "keeills" (cells) of the Isle of Man, and the "kils" of Ireland and Scotland.

The dedication patterns of these llans strongly suggest the efforts of individual saints radiating out by sea, or by ancient trackways and Roman roads, from the larger centres. In some places, their tiny cells were

built in or near some conspicuous deserted site such as a Roman or prehistoric ruin. A spring or well, perhaps already venerated by pagans, would be a prime target for takeover, and would continue to serve a sacred purpose in the sacrament of baptism, as well as being of practical everyday use. All the sites would have been isolated as there was little or nothing in the way of towns or villages throughout Wales. Nearly half of the sites are still quite isolated. We can imagine that, just like African missions and their outlying stations at the present day, some became a tiny nucleus of settlement within the scattered population. Some are in fact now the sites of hamlets and villages, and a few are swamped by large towns. Many have later churches built over the original site. Some are still recognised only by an adjacent well or spring still bearing the name of the saint. Were these sites intended as retreats or for pastoral care? Possibly both. Each one represented an individual endeavour that still speaks to us over the centuries. Most people in Wales live in or near a place commemorating in this way the name of a saint and are thus daily reminded of a sacred past.

In passing, mention must be made of a curious and significant fact. After a while, the visitor, however casual, to these sites cannot fail to be struck by their evocative beauty, a beauty which returns unbidden to haunt the memory and enrich the spirit.

Now I have no desire to start a contest between them! But an interested visitor could well begin, for the sake of example, with the sites of the two dedications to Celynin. The ancient church of Llancelynin north of Towyn lies tucked away on the coast between the road and the railway request halt and enjoys views over much of Cardigan Bay. Many do pause and stop in this beautiful place. The other Llancelynin stands within a stone rath at an altitude of a thousand feet, as the crow flies just a bare three miles southwest of Conwy. I

would guess, however, that scarcely one in ten thousand of the numerous visitors to Conwy ever comes to this Llancelynin. If they did, they could travel on a route marked by menhirs already two thousand years old when the Romans built their (still visible) road there, passing cromlechs and stone circles in an ancient landscape of Celtic fields overlooked by a hill fort with a cheveaux-des-frises.

Again, one might visit Llantecwyn, standing alone above its charming lake and looking out over the beautiful sandy joint estuary of the Glaslyn and Dwyryd. In Anglesey one might visit the chapel dedicated to Cwyfan on an island in a sandy bay, or the ruined church at Llanddwyn, the Celtic saint of lovers, situated on a tidewashed peninsula looking out towards the hills of Lleyn and the pilgrim route to Bardsey, a view unrivalled when seen in the light of a late summer evening. One might pass by Llansadwrn and marvel how among all the notable views of Snowdonia from

this part of Anglesey, Sadwrn got his site just right at the point where rocky Tryfan peeps dramatically round the Carneddau. Anglesey, incidentally, has some sixty-seven sites dedicated to Celtic saints, the densest pattern in the whole of Wales.

One could quietly go to visit any selection of them or indeed, for that matter, any in Wales. The visitor and observer will, eventually, come away with more than a view to remember, and will return ever if only in thoughts. Who could, for example, visit the secret valley of Pennant, verdant with wild flowers, the lonely chapel inside its rath encircled by enormous ancient yews, and ever forget the associated legend of Melangell with its core of essential truth: man is part of nature, neither more nor less.

But the land was poor. Resources in rural Wales were minimal. There was nothing that could be called a town until Norman times. There were no great scriptoria. No breathtaking illuminated manuscripts have come down to us. As we have noted in passing, very little remains in the way of buildings attributable to this period. Three or four bronze handbells have survived over the thirteen centuries or so from the time when they were among the few prized personal possessions of the saints. I have seen one, partly corroded, hanging on a length of baling wire in a remote chapel. It was retrieved with some difficulty by the local people from the National Museum in Cardiff. After all, it was theirs. But do they fully realise, I sometimes wonder, just how much of a priceless and almost unique relic it represents? What is perhaps more common, as a tangible reminder of a founding saint, is a simple cross inscribed on a stone in a churchyard, often poignantly with no name.

And that is it, at least superficially. But one thing that the Age of Saints may have fostered in Wales is an ongoing tradition of learning and spirituality, coupled with an artistic sense, particularly in oral traditions of poetry and singing. And do we not see in all of this also some lingering folk memory of the strong oral tradition of the Celt? These activities could readily be carried on in the setting of a lonely farmhouse, where a family and friends could gather. Celtic tradition indeed runs strong in the 14th-century poetry of Dafydd ap Gwilym. Under a great yew in the grounds of remote Strata Florida abbey there is a simple tribute to him – "the earliest of the great singers of wild nature in medieval Europe". Fortunately, Wales still has her local and national eisteddfoddau, now joined by the popular annual international eisteddfod.

Travel, if you will, to Ty Mawr, the lonely 16th-century farmhouse in the hidden and little-visited upland valley of Wybrnant in North Wales, alive with summer song-birds, where Bishop William Morgan spent his childhood, and to the remote valley of Llanrhaeadr-ym-mochnant (the Christian settlement by the waterfall in the valley of the swine), situated on an old droving route and hidden in the Berwyn mountains, where he was priest. Marvel that, working alone,

he was the first to translate the whole Bible into Welsh. Its publication in 1588, as well as making the scriptures more readily available to all Welsh people, was an enormous inducement to literacy and to the preservation of Welsh language. It was an apt riposte to the Act of Annexation (1535) that set out to "extirp" the Welsh language and culture.

Or travel again, if you will, to the ruined cottage at Llanfihangel-y-pennant at the head of the Dysynni valley below Cader Idris, passing as you go the amazing Craig Aderyn and the ruins of Castell-y-Bere, the last stronghold of Llywelyn. Marvel that from this lonely place two centuries ago, Mary Jones, a young girl of sixteen, having somehow saved some pennies, walked alone over the mountains to the north all the way to Bala to buy a Welsh Bible. The minister there, Thomas Charles, had none left, but he was so touched that he gave her his own and inscribed it – it has been preserved and can now be seen in Cambridge University library. Later, as a direct result of Mary's quest, Charles was inspired to found the British and Foreign Bible Society, which to date has distributed hundreds of millions of Bibles in 140 tongues throughout the world.

The power of individual endeavour is undying – our most precious renewable resource in fact. This lesson is indeed one the Celtic heritage of the Age of Saints teaches us abundantly,

The Isle of Man, Cornwall, Brittany, even Galicia in northwest Spain, also knew well the Age of Saints. Their history at this time runs somewhat parallel to that of Wales. I hope they will pardon me for not alluding to them in detail. Brittany, in particular, deserves fuller mention. Reinforced by migration from Britain, she attained a considerable population of 300,000 by the 7th century, a viable base which enabled her to maintain her Celtic traditions and indeed her independence from France for centuries. But there is one area we have so far omitted any detailed reference to and should now move on to consider, a land that was to prove pre-eminent in the history of the Celtic church: Ireland.

Christianity had reached Erin's shores before Patrick. It is said that Ninian himself visited Ireland from Galloway as a missionary in the late 4th century, and it is known that Gaulish Christians arrived in southeastern Ireland early in the 5th century. Tradition preserves the names of four pre-Patrician bishops: Ailbhe of Emly, Ibar of Wexford Harbour, Declan of Ardmore, and Kieran of Saigir. It is recorded that Pope Celestine sent Palladius to minister to established Christian communities in Ireland in 431. Very little else is known, however, and it is to Patrick, "Magonus Sucatus Patricius" (died 461?, 493?, dates seriously disputed) that we justifiably look for a strong acceleration in the acceptance of Christianity throughout Ireland. And it is to Patrick's own accounts, in the form of a short biography and a letter to a colleague in England, that we can turn for a fascinating glimpse of Irish people and their pre-literate Iron Age society.

Patrick's story is improbable but true. Raiding Irish had carried him off aged fifteen from his home in western Britain. He then worked in Ireland as a slave (or "unfree man", see below) herding cows for six years. He managed to escape on a boat to Gaul, where he studied first at Lérins and then under Germanus at Auxerre, before returning to Britain, possibly at or close to the time of Germanus's first visit to Britain in 429. Then in ·432 (possibly later) Patrick made the fateful decision to return to Ireland, the land of his previous captivity, with the modest aim of converting its entire people to Christianity. This, amazingly, was achieved to a large degree. This success was no doubt due as much to his enforced familiarity with Irish language and customs as to his own convictions and ability. After landing in the north near the mouth of Strangford Lough he worked steadily inland. Although he always bemoaned his lack of an adequate classical education, Patrick (probably shortly helped by others) succeeded in making Latin the language of the church in Ireland. He made Armagh his see and, eventually, after many adventures, established a diocesan organisation throughout much of Ireland. Significantly, the dioceses were based perforce on tribal areas.

Celtic society in Ireland, virtually untouched by Roman influence as we have mentioned, was tribal and comprised chieftains, druids, warriors, freemen, and slaves. Successors to chieftains came from the ruling family but not necessarily according to rules of primogeniture. On the contrary, the best potential leader was chosen by the tribe, ideally by acclamation. Herein lay a fertile possible source of conflict. It would appear that warriors were not slow to take up arms both in such internal conflicts and, more commonly, in the traditional sport of cattle raiding. The freemen typically owned cattle and a share of any arable land and also included craftsmen, notably blacksmiths and other metal workers. Cattle were the traditional form of wealth (just as brideprice and other payments in parts of Africa today are denominated in cattle). A fit slave woman (cumal), for example, was worth three milch cows or six heifers. Slaves, more accurately unfree rather than slaves, included prisoners, criminals, and cowards. They had no franchise in tribal affairs and had no right to bear arms.

A fascinating glimpse into the heroics of this kind of Iron Age society is given in two surviving sagas. The first, the Ulster Cycle, refers to events taking place around the 1st century A.D. They concern the warriors of King Conchober of Ulster, of whom the foremost was Cú Chulainn. The subtitles themselves give some idea of the contents: Cattle Raid of Cooley, Mac Datho's Pig, The Feast of Bricriu, Drunkenness of the Ulstermen, Tragedy of Deirdriu, Exile of the Sons of Uisiu. The later 3rd-century Fenian Cycle records, inter alia, the first Irish raids on Roman Britain.

The controversial term "druid" encompassed those whom we can attempt to itemise and describe as follows:

1. Bards (filidh), who spent a very long period, as much as twelve to twenty years, of rigorous training and testing in the oral traditions of history, genealogy, and ongoing annals of the tribe (such as the abovementioned sagas), repeated in verse form. Such long training was, of course, essential if this kind of knowledge were to be preserved and handed down accurately from generation to generation, as all were illiterate. The memory work involved was phenomenal. Some bards, however, might more aptly be described as mere sycophantic praise-poets (bardai), and were retained to sing the exaggerated praises of the local chief at feasts. It is interesting to note that secular bardic

schools persisted in Ireland until the 17th century.

2. Lawyers (brehons), who had similarly acquired a thorough working knowledge of the common law of the tribe.

3. Soothsayers, similar to shamans in other primitive societies today, in touch with the spirits of the departed, and co-ordinators of rites held at sacred places. These druids were held to be capable of magical powers and foretelling the future, frequently in conjunction with interpretation of omens and with sacrificial rites, some of them unpleasant, held at sacred sites such as lakes and oak groves.

4. Doctors, with medicinal skills and knowledge of bone-setting, herbal remedies, and spiritual healing.

5. A soul-friend (anmchara) of the chieftain, relied upon for spiritual guidance and confidential impartial advice. "A leader without a soul-friend is a body without a head" (Comgall).

No doubt, at times, some of these functions, involving the knowledgable, the poetic, the judicial, the magical, the terrible, the practical, and the avuncular, overlapped in one individual. Merlin (Myrddin), a familiar druid of legend, indeed assumes these disconcertingly different guises in different stories and situations. Some kind of a parallel could perhaps be drawn with the Brahmans of Hindu India. Like them, the druids tended to form hereditary castes.

It would seem that the first Christian missionaries were tentatively, perhaps even readily, accepted into tribal society as a kind of ancillary druid with some powerful and ready answers to such eternal questions as the mystery of creation, life on earth, and the hereafter. Some, including Patrick himself, became involved in personal rivalries with established druids. Some became the soul-friends of chieftains. Patrick, for example, became the soul-friend of King Loeghaire. Brynach Wyddel (Brynach the Irishman) was the soul-friend ("periglor" in Welsh) of the King Brychan in Wales of whom we have spoken already. Even a century later, Columba was the soul-friend of King Aidan of Dalraida and we know, from Columba's own account, of leading Christians being part of and party to tribal conflicts.

So all in all it was a pretty rough scene – very different indeed from the relatively sophisticated ambience of the classical world onto which Christianity was grafted – but perhaps not all that distance removed from the more primitive pastoral and agricultural society of Galilee where the ideas and teaching of Christ germinated.

Then something quite momentous happened. In relation to the number of total population, monasticism took a hold on Ireland as in no other country of Christendom. Patrick's see, Armagh, itself seems to have become monastic as early as the end of the 5th century. Furthermore, the intimate environment of tribal society apparently initially favoured the establishment of hereditary monastic Christian druids, married and with families, in each tribe. In Ireland, where monasticism developed a little later than in Wales, we are fortunate in having not only tangible remains on a considerable number of sites but also writings to corroborate our knowledge of the history of development of this important branch of the Celtic church. Nevertheless, it must be admitted that the precise details of its beginnings are shrouded in uncertainty.

One of the earliest monastic foundations in Ireland is also certainly the most enigmatic. This is the nunnery said to have been founded by Brigid, "Mary of the Gaels" (c.450–c.523) in Kildare (church of the oak). Reliable accounts of this unusual female establishment are not available. Furthermore, much of the material that has come down to us concerning Brigid herself clearly belongs more in the realms of folklore and myth. In these tales it would seem that Brigid (alias Brigit) has assumed much of the persona of a Celtic fertility goddess of the same name, cognate with the Sanskrit Brhati, "the exalted one". Significantly, in the Christian calendar the Feast Day of St. Brigid is the same as Imbolc, as mentioned above, the Celtic feast to do with lambing and lactation. Brigid was herself the daughter of a powerful pagan nobleman and had been fostered and educated in the home of a druid.

We would seem therefore to be witnessing in Brigid the transition from Celtic to Christian society. However, the more one learns and thinks about it, the more it seems that this may not have been a matter of the *conversion* of the Irish, but rather the *incorporation of Christian beliefs and practices into an already sophisticated druid society*. Dedications to Brigid are numerous and widespread, not only throughout Ireland, but also in Wales, Cornwall, Scotland, Cumbria, Wirral, and Brittany.

Another very early monastic foundation is Monasterboice, famous for its Cross of Muiredach, perhaps the most perfect High Cross in Ireland, dated to the early 10th century. Monasterboice was founded by a little-known saint called Buite, who is said to have died in 521. His monastery endured until the 11th century. There are several other monastic foundations reputed to be of early 6th-century date about which little is known in any detail.

We seem to be more in the documented mainstream of monastic development with Enda (died c.530). Enda learnt the principles of monastic life in Britain. Precisely where is not stated, but it is inferred to be probably Whithorn. Enda founded what is frequently said to have been the first male monastery in Ireland on Aranmore, the largest of the Aran Islands in Galway Bay. His rule was strict and severe. Ciaran (see below) was among Enda's pupils .

Other accounts say that the first true monastery was the famous foundation of Finnian (died of plague c.549) at Clonard in c.530 on the site of one of Patrick's churches. Certainly, Clonard quickly grew to become the largest and most renowned teaching institution in Ireland in the 6th century, comparable to, and eventually surpassing, Llanilltud in Wales. Perhaps its very fame has come to usurp Enda's, Buite's, and others' claims to being earlier. We are told that Finnian proceeded "in the light of the teaching of Cadog and Gildas". Among Finnian's pupils were the so-called "Twelve Apostles of Ireland", including notably Ciaran, Brendan, and Columba.

Ciaran (c.516–49) founded Clonmacnoise in 541 at the place where the route of the ancient chariot road across Ireland crosses the Shannon. He had received his training at both Aranmore and Clonard and thus ranks as the first documented home-grown Irish abbot. Despite his tragic early death also in the plague, his foundation of Clonmacnoise thrived and was to become another renowned centre of learning and to endure for centuries. Alcuin himself came to study there under Colgu the Wise. Evocative ruins (of later buildings on the same site) persist to this day, and are a beloved place of visitation by Irish people and others. Clonmacnoise is justly famed for its tradition of preservation in writing of Irish folk tales and mythology. The *Book of the Dun Cow*, one of the most ancient secular Irish manuscripts extant and an important source of Irish legends and myths, was compiled at Clonmacnoise. The famous 11th-century annalist Tighernach studied here. An analogy can be made with the comparable interest taken, much later, in Welsh affairs and traditions by the Cistercian foundation of Strata Florida in central Wales. The Cistercians, like the Celtic monks, sought out the wilder places and in their way of life were distinct from the worldly Benedictines, imposed on Wales by the Normans and detested by the Welsh people.

Brendan (486–578) was another notable student of Finnian's, after having been instructed as a young boy in the nunnery of Ita in Killeedy, County Limerick. His foundation of Clonfert, County Galway in 563 was to endure to the 16th century. Brendan, "the Voyager", was certainly a noted traveller. He visited Brittany and explored the Western Isles of Scotland. But whether he personally visited Iceland and made a landfall in the Americas, as is claimed in his Life, is doubtful. Some Irish monks did settle in Iceland, which they accurately described as a land light enough at midnight in summer to see to pick nits out of their hair, and it is recorded in Norse Sagas that Irish priests were indeed discovered there and duly massacred. Just off the northeast coast of Newfoundland is a small group of islands known collectively as St. Brendan's. This cannot of course reflect an ongoing tradition, but is rather a fanciful (but inspired?) naming.

Finnian's most famous student, and one who is central to our story was Columba (521–97), also known as Colmcille. He studied first under Finnian of Moville (see below) before going to Clonard. Columba was the son of a chieftain and a great-grandson of Niall of the Nine Hostages, High King of Ireland. He seems to have inherited a proud and quarrelsome disposition, as we shall see. Columba's first own foundation was at Derry in 546 inside the walls of an old fort given to him by his cousin, Chief Aedh. Several more important foundations by Columba followed in the period 546 to 563. These include the famous monasteries of Durrow and Kells. Durrow is of course well known in connection with one of the earliest extant illuminated manuscripts. The Book of Durrow, which rests proudly today next to the Book of Kells in Trinity College, Dublin, is a small book of the gospels almost certainly copied in Lindisfarne as it uses a very pure rendering of St. Jerome's Vulgate that was brought to Northumberland from Rome. It may well have come to Ireland at the time Colman left Lindisfarne following the Synod of Whitby (see below) in 664.

The site of Kells, originally granted to Columba in the mid 6th century for the foundation of a monastery, was probably re-founded in 804 on the occasion of return of monks from Iona, following repeated sackings of Iona in Viking raids. Kells itself was sacked in 919, 950, and 969. The Book of Kells was retrieved from a field nearby. It had probably been writtten, or at least begun (it is in several hands) in Iona at the end of the 8th century.

Finnian of Moville (died c.579), not to be confused with Finnian of Clonard, was, like the latter, British trained. He was a student at Whithorn in Galloway, where he got into trouble over a Pictish girl. He fled to Ireland where he founded a monastery at Moville in 540. This became a highly regarded school, relatively very well stocked for the times in Latin texts from Rome. It was the infamous quarrel over surreptitious copying of a Latin Gospel belonging to Finnian that led to Columba eventually being exiled and departing in high dudgeon to Iona, with the far-reaching consequences that no one could have foreseen at the time. Judgement on the matter had been given by the High King Diarmuid himself who pronounced that the copy belonged like a calf to its mother cow, i.e., not to the copier (Columba) but to the owner of the original (Finnian). Columba's selfish and headstrong refusal to hand back the copy that he had made led to a bloody tribal battle and eventually to his banishment. The whole story could well be apocryphal but, in passing, one notes the very high value put upon manuscripts.

Not far from Moville lies the monastery of Bangor on Belfast Lough, founded by Comgall (517–603) in c.577. Bangor was to become one of the greatest Irish monastic centres before it was destroyed by the Vikings in 823. "Saints and scholars, not buildings, were its glory." Three well-known saints who were later to establish monasteries in Scotland received their training at Bangor: Moluag of (the Scottish) Lismore, who was reputed to have founded a hundred monasteries in Pictland; Meaelrubha of Applecross, who in the 7th century paralleled the achievements of Columba and Moluag in the 6th; and Blane of Dunblane and Bute.

Comgall himself founded a monastery in Tiree where he lived for a while.

The evangelisation of mainland Britain beginning in Scotland was a very important, one could well say the most important, step in ending the Dark Ages in western Europe, and we shall shortly return to this subject. Bangor also nurtured Columbanus and Gall, of whom also more anon.

One could go on reciting from a long list of Irish saints and their foundations. We will just mention one more, that of Kevin (d.618) at Glendalough. In spite of being the most popular site visited by tourists in Ireland, this beautiful place manages to retain an evocative flavour, best appreciated, one has to say, alone in the early morning or in the evening. A boat trip on the lake and a short but steep climb are necessary to reach the stone foundations of a very early hermitage (Kevin's?) situated some distance away from the complex of later buildings.

By the end of the sixth century, what one might call the heroic epoch in the age of Irish saints, there came to be over sixty monasteries in Ireland. Clonard was the largest with a reputed 3,000 monks and auxiliaries. Some monasteries were very much smaller, with perhaps only a dozen denizens, the average perhaps being a few score. In aggregate, they represented an enormous investment by a fairly primitive society that comprised no more than a few hundred thousand people.

The early foundations consisted of a rath, a more or less circular enclosure typically surrounded by an earthen ditch and rampart and probably fenced. This contained an oblong oratory and individual round houses for the monks and their families. The usual building materials were wattle and daub and thatch, sometimes hewn planks for the oratory, except where stone was readily available.

Amazingly, an example, just one, has come down to us virtually intact. It is situated near the top of the dif-

ficultly accessible precipitous pinnacle of the island of Skellig Michael, which rises improbably seven hundred feet above the stormy Atlantic seven miles offshore from the tip of the Kerry peninsula. This small monastery comprised two oratories, six beehive huts (clochans) and a well. A grave plot contains small slabs with incised crosses. It was all built of stone (of which there is no shortage on Skellig) and there have been no settlers since to rob it for its stone, and no frosts to damage its structures. Tiny terraced gardens were laboriously built by the monks and earth gathered for them. The date of the monastery is unknown – 7th century might be a reasonable guess. Like several other small monastic settlements, not as well preserved, to be found among the western islands and headlands of Ireland (notably Inishmurray approximately twelve miles northwest of Sligo, and Inishglora off the Mullet peninsula, County Mayo), it must have served as a retreat.

In contrast to these awe-inspiring retreats, the larger monastic settlements came to be much more in the nature of small townships, each under the rule of a powerful hereditary succession of abbots. In addition to cells and oratories, their buildings came to comprise guest houses, schools, and a refectory. They provided accommodation for students, wayfarers, widows, orphans, the infirm and aged, even retired kings and queens. Bede recounts that many Englishmen of his time received their education in Ireland and that the Irish monks "welcomed all kindly, and, without asking for any payment, provided them with daily food, books, and instruction."

These larger settlements were not just monastic and scholastic communities but were eminently practical. They were centres of craftmanship and employed over-all a large number of people such as farmers, tanners, carpenters, smiths, jewellers, masons, millers, brewers, weavers, bakers, nurses, scribes and librarians, in addition to scholars and priests and their families. Many of these larger monastic settlements were in agriculturally rich and productive areas, quite unlike the austere retreats.

Clearly, at this stage of development, the larger monasteries were self-sufficient and could offer a parallel way of life to that of traditional tribal society, with an increasing emphasis on a settled agrarian economy rather than a pastoral one. Given the conditions of the time, they must have seemed very attractive places in which to live. Monasteries became so important in fact that the Laws of Ireland at one time came to define the relationship between the "tribe of the people" and the "tribe of the church".

What is more, letters and learning came to be highly valued. This learning came to include not just study of the Scriptures but also of some of the classics in both Latin and Greek. Irish mastery of the classics came to exceed that anywhere in Roman Europe. Not only this, some of the Irish monastic institutions also fostered the preservation of Irish bardic legends, genealogies, and folk tales. For example, the earliest written version of the Ulster Cycle, alluded to above, was in fact written by a monk of Clonmacnoise. The earliest Irish historian to commit events to writing may have been Sinlan Moccu Min (d.607), an abbot of (the Irish) Bangor, who added a chronology of Irish historical events to a copy of the Latin Chronology of Eusebius.

Several of the monasteries contained important scriptoria where manuscripts were laboriously copied by hand, using quills and parchment. The Christian manuscripts typically included numerous working copies of the Gospels, New Testament, Psalms, and penal codes. These were hung up in tooled leather satchels (tiag liubhair) which are often portrayed in stone carvings. The more elaborate illustrated manuscripts would have served as ceremonial works, housed in a bejewelled casket, kept in a place of honour and used only at important services in leading monasteries. As far as we know, no equivalent to the great Irish scriptoria existed in Wales on any comparable scale. It should be remarked, however, that the transmission of Latin to previously illiterate Irish Celts was in itself a notable achievement of the Britons and Gauls.

By the 8th century, it could truly be said that a Heroic Age had given place to a Golden Age of Irish monastic civilisation. Tangible records of achievement include:

(i) the great illuminated manuscripts that have come down to us,

(ii) metalwork of great beauty and intricacy, producing chalices, reliquaries, hanging-bowls, brooches, etc. in bronze and precious metals, frequently incorporating centuries-old Celtic themes, and

(iii) the beginnings of sculpture (some copying metalwork in stone) that was to culminate after two centuries of development in the incomparable High Crosses of Ireland, of which nearly three hundred remain.

Examples of all these artistic achievements can be seen and admired today by any casual visitor to Ireland. But all this was not the most important product of Ireland's Golden Age. Two other things were.

The first was people. Well-trained literate Irish monks were to wander and, after "seeking a solitude in the pathless sea", to evangelise the whole of western Europe. They travelled as far north as Iceland, as far south as Taranto in southern Italy, and as far east as Kiev. We shall document some of this later.

The second, perhaps more subtle, involved the protection of the filidh by the Celtic church and the development of Irish language and secular writing and poetry, leading to the preservation of Celtic traditions in writing. Irish is of course the only other ancient vernacular language committed to writing in western Europe besides Latin and Greek. All this amounted to not just a tangible record of a vanished *way* of life, but also the preservation of the living Celtic *view* of life involving, among other facets, *a manifest love of Nature and all Creation.*

This preservation of the history and myths of an Iron

Age society has its parallels in Homer, the recorders of Indian myths, and Old Testamant scribes. Like them, it represents a priceless part of the human heritage on earth. Just as the lovely islands and the surrounding mountains and coastal plains of the Aegean nurtured the Iliad and the Odyssey, and the vast timeless plains of India nurtured the Vedas, and the once fertile Levant nurtured the books of the Old Testament, so the misty and scenic peninsulas and islands of the Celtic west nurtured the surviving sagas of Irish mythology and folk tales.

To varying degrees, each of the above provides a unique and enduring insight into the psychic roots of mankind. It is this kind of insight that must have vividly informed all those who participated in the Age of Saints in Ireland. And it is, eventually, this insight which, to some degree, will rub off on the visitor and inspire the seeker.

Postscript: But although they may still speak to us across the centuries, Golden Ages themselves, alas, have a habit of not enduring. Sometimes the danger comes from within. We can infer that the noble asceticism of the Heroic Age had in fact succumbed in some degree to relative luxury and complacency by the Golden Age. But a greater danger to Ireland came from without.

Two centuries of Viking raids began in 795 with the sacking of a monastic settlement on the island of Lambay near Dublin, and continued unabated throughout much of the 9th century. After a lull between 880 and 914, Viking attacks resumed.

Some 120 round towers (almost unique to Ireland; there are two in Scotland and one in the Isle of Man), nearly all in monastic settlements, reflect the desperate attempts of the Irish to protect themselves. They were built mainly during the 10th century. Ardmore, the last, was built in the 12th century. Although they may well have served a secondary purpose as belfreys where monks could ring their handbells from the top, they are clearly defensive in design. They are high (Scattery, the tallest, is 120 feet high), sturdily built, and have doorways twelve to fifteen feet above ground level. Thirteen remain in virtually pristine condition to this day, all silent witnesses to an age of rapine.

There were great losses in people and material. To give just one poignant example, Clonmacnoise, the jewel of Irish learning, was plundered and burnt no fewer than ten times by marauding invaders.

All this was not before the Irish mission (see below) had taken firm root overseas. Indeed, much of what we know of Ireland's Golden Age comes from surviving manuscripts preserved in continental "Irish" monasteries. We can also infer that fear of the Vikings was to become a potent factor behind the continuing migration of Irish monks to the continent.

Eventually the Viking invaders settled down and prospered in their trading cities of Dublin, Wexford, Waterford, Cork and Limerick, adopted Christianity, and became less dangerous. In any event, their power was finally broken by the decisive battle of Clontarf, 1014, fought near Dublin.

The final chapter, very long and very miserable, of the Irish story was begun by the Plantagenets in 1169. Under the infamous sanction given to them by Pope

Adrian IV (an Englishman), under Henry II of England they invaded and conquered Ireland and saw to it, inter alia, that the Celtic church was replaced by a Roman one. To give but one instance, their repeated plunderings reduced the great Clonmacnoise, which amazingly had recovered from all the Viking raids, to poverty and obscurity. Then followed a very sordid story of nearly eight centuries of English oppression, land-grabbing, and exploitation of the people of "England's first colony". The worst actual massacres of Irish people, after the initial 12th-century onslaught, were in the times of Elizabeth, Cromwell, and William of Orange. The greatest widespread misery of the native Irish population, however, was probably during the time of the fiendishly discriminatory 18th-century Penal Codes extending up to the time of the famines in the 1840s. The whole forms an appalling story that was certainly glossed over in my school history books and is probably not familiar in detail to many British people.

As well as ignorance, does one detect twinges of suppressed conscience or just plain arrogance in prevalent English attitudes towards the Irish and other Celtic minorities even to this day? These attitudes, it seems to me, need to be addressed. For the irony, as we shall see, is that England, a land of benighted and befuddled savages, in large measure owed its civilisation to the Irish. Let us also not forget that Britain was never better than when Celt and Saxon worked together (see below). Hopefully, sanity and peace will eventually prevail.

VI   MISSION

The Irish evangelisation and education of mainland
Britain and western Europe is indeed an amazing
story. The two processes naturally went hand in hand
at a time when the only literate places were the monasteries.

The story begins with the settlement of some Irish
people (the Scots) on the mainland of Argyll and its offshore islands in the district known as Dalraida from
498 onwards. A succession of Irish kings had their
stronghold at Dunadd, a prominent isolated hill
strategically situated on a narrow part of the Kintyre
peninsula. Irish monastic settlements followed in
their wake. The ruined beehive huts of a very early
Irish monastic site can still be seen on the most
southerly of the Garvellach Isles.

It was to another island, Iona, that Columba, along
with some companion monks, came in 565, after first
landing in Jura in 563. The circumstances of Columba's departure from Ireland were, as mentioned above,
ignominious, one could say disgraceful, if accounts are
to be believed. His arrival in Iona was certainly not
welcomed by Oran, the leader of a community of Irish
monks already established there. Columba's fiery reputation had preceded him. He was no "dove". But then

achievers are not necessarily always the nicest people. From these unpropitious beginnings Iona flourished, indeed became easily pre-eminent, and we know of many other Iona-based monastic settlements in the Hebrides and expeditions beyond, such as the one led by Cormac to Orkney, Faroe, and Iceland. Columba was to remain based on Iona for 32 years until his death. Constant traffic plied between Ireland and Iona and adjacent parts, it has been said via a "bridge of cur- rachs", following a route in the lee of Colonsay and through the Sound of Islay, with several safe havens at hand if conditions were bad.

From Iona, Columba took his mission to an enigmatic tribal people – the Picts of eastern Scotland. He
met the Pictish King Bruide at the latter's hill fort just
outside Inverness. After initial coolness a few converts
were made, maybe even the king himself, although evidence of this is conflicting. More likely, some kind of an
accommodation was reached whereby Columba was
granted asylum for his activities (the Picts and Scots
had only recently been at war).

Now the above may all appeaar to be somewhat
peripheral to Europe. The Celtic peoples, be they
British or Irish, were, to put it mildly, not friends with
the English. Any expanding missionary activity of the
Celtic church might therefore well have been geographically confined by an insuperable racial barrier.
But now our story takes an unexpected twist. Via Iona,
a bridge was made between Celt and English. The setting for this historic event was Lindisfarne in
Northumbria. But before considering this, we must
first look at events in England.

In the year 597, coincidentally the year of Columba's
death in faraway misty Iona, Augustine arrived in
Kent. He had been despatched from Rome by Pope Gregory to convert the heathen and uncivilised English.
This was a prospect so daunting that Augustine and
his men had turned back once. Reading Bede's account
of it all, one is irresistibly reminded of Gilbert and Sul-
livan's constables. Two things convinced them to
change their mind. The first was relentless prodding
by their boss, Gregory. The second was the arranged
marriage of the savage and pagan Kentish King Ethelbert to a Christian Frankish lady who, as a condition of
marriage to this unprepossessing gentleman, had

insisted on bringing a Christian chaplain with her from Gaul to Kent. This provided Augustine and his colleagues with an introduction. No doubt the good lady urged her husband to entertain them. The first meeting of King Ethelbert with Augustine's group was held in the open air as the King was suspicious of Christian witchcraft.

The mission of Augustine had some initial success. Ethelbert was duly converted and baptized. He even issued a code of laws making it clear that the new Christian church was to enjoy royal protection. Bishops were appointed in Canterbury, Rochester, and London. Augustine's mission deserves some praise for its achievements although, as we have noted, Augustine failed to reach any accommodation with the British church. But overall it was a halting affair, although it is often the point at which English histories like to begin their account of Christian England. It was confined to Kent, Sussex and, precariously, in Essex, where the savage King Redwald (the one probably buried with the famous Sutton Hoo treasure) hedged his bets by having two parallel altars, one devoted to pagan Gods and one to Christ.

After the deaths of Augustine in 609 and of King Ethelbert in 616, much of the nominally converted area of southeastern England reverted to paganism. Bishop Mellitus, for example, was driven out of London. Perhaps Augustine spoke more to princes than to people?

Now our story moves decisively to Northumbria. After the Northumbrian King Ethelfrith's bloody victories over the British at Chester and elsewhere, he had established Northumbria as a powerful kingdom extending from the Irish Sea to the North Sea, between the Humber to the south and the narrow land frontier between the Forth and Clyde to the north. Ethelfrith himself was slain on his southern frontier in 616 by Redwald (by now thoroughly pagan again). Ethelfrith was succeeded by Edwin during whose reign an era of peace and stability was initiated in Northumbria. Edwin was converted to Christianity in 627 by a mission from Canterbury led by Paulinus. In a tactic reminiscent of Augustine's, Paulinus had accompanied Edwin's Kentish and Christian bride, Ethelburga, in 619. But in 633 Edwin was defeated and killed by a combined force of Mercians under Penda and North Welsh under Cadwallon, an unlikely but expedient alliance in an era of unprincipled tribal warfare. Following Edwin's death, Paulinus fled south never to return, and Northumbria relapsed into paganism and anarchy.

The situation in Northumbria was saved by Oswald. Oswald, a scion of a sub-province of Northumbria, had wisely fled with several companions during the troubles to, of all places, Iona, where they had been given hospitality by the monks and had learnt Irish. Following a triumphant return to Northumbria in 634 Oswald defeated and killed Cadwallon at a site called Heavenfield near Hexham. Before the battle he had erected a Christian cross and called upon the Christian God for support in his fight against (the Christian) Cadwallon.

Soon after the successful outcome of this battle Oswald sent for an Irish monk of Iona, Aidan, to come and help reconvert his country to Christianity. Northumbria then witnessed the extraordinary spectacle of a humble Irish monk travelling throughout the land proclaiming the Christian message translated by, of all people, their own king at his side. This was pretty powerful stuff and it was successful. One would have to say that it was very different indeed from the spectacle of timorous Latin priests clinging to the petticoats of king's womenfolk. Tragically, Oswald, the first Englisher to be canonised, was later killed at a battle near Oswestry (Oswald's tree) in 642 by Penda, the great pagan Mercian king. The debilitating tribal warfare between Northumbria and Mercia was only finally ended by the decisive victory of Oswald's brother Oswy over Penda in 655 at Winwaed near Leeds.

Meanwhile, Aidan had established a notable Celtic monastery on the Holy Isle of Lindisfarne, a tidal island off the Northumbrian coast. It attracted many more Irish monks and fostered a truly remarkable stable of English ones including Cuthbert, Chad, and Cedd. The link between Celt and English was thus forged here. It was to prove overwhelmingly important. "Augustine was the apostle of Kent, but Aidan was the apostle of England." How true. We know of all this in accurate detail thanks to the great historical work of Bede on the history of the English church and people completed by him in 731, four years before his death.

A few words about Bede (c.673–735). He was a most learned man and most thoroughly deserves his unique epithet of "venerable". His thirty-four volumes include works ranging from exegesis to biography, and from history to science. He was interested in all kinds of natural phenomena and, for example, closely observed the tides and the stars with a true scientist's interest. He was and is, of course, best known for his *History*, which remained for many centuries the most copied secular work throughout Europe in the Dark Ages and early Middle Ages. He wrote in a very clear and precise Latin (unlike the more flowery style of some of the Celts!) and this style never fails to come across in translation. His qualities as a historian are characterised by his establishment of the AD system of precise dates, and by his insistence on clear identification of sources and indications of their relative trustworthiness. His quality as a man is characterised by his great charity towards the Irish monks (who had been severely discomfited by the result of the Synod of Whitby; see below) and acknowledgement of Northumbria's debt to them. Bede speaks of Aidan in these terms: "Saint Aidan was a man of remarkable gentleness, goodness, and moderation, zealous for God; but not", Bede felt constrained to add, "fully according to knowledge . . ." (knowledge according to the Roman church, that is; see below).

Bede includes in his history and biographies some unforgettable vignettes such as the pagan priest Coifi's comparison of a sparrow's brief flight through a warm lighted hall being like our own brief mortal lives on earth, the touching story of the humble cowman Caedmon who had the gift of poetry, and the departure for Rome of the elderly Abbot Ceolfrith (Bede's mentor) and his party carrying the great Amiatinus Bible, watched by the weeping brethren from the shore. Ceolfrith never made it, as intended, to the Pope in Rome; he died en route at Langres, Burgundy. Half of his party returned with his body. The others struggled on to Italy, only to have the great Bible stolen from them by Italian monks. The Bible, produced in the scriptorium of Lindisfarne and claimed to be the oldest surviving complete Latin Bible in the world, is still in a library in Florence.

Bede's shining example of scholarship and his personal interest led to the subsequent emergence of York for a time as the greatest library in Christendom. Alcuin was nurtured there and went on to become the most eminent adviser at Charlemagne's court, where he was nicknamed the "schoolmaster" of Carolingian Renaissance Europe. The monastery church of Jarrow where Bede worked still stands bearing the dedication stone, dated 685 and mentioning Abbot Ceolfrith, that Bede must often have looked at.

Two things about Bede never cease to amaze me. First, that the foremost scholar of all Europe in his time and certainly not equalled at least until the 12th century, among other achievements a man very arguably the greatest historian Britain has ever produced, should have been descended from savages a mere generation or two previously. And, second, that he was never mentioned to me in my conventional English education! Why? Because he was only someone in the (so-called) Dark Ages!

It is of course very possible that we tend to ascribe prominence to Lindisfarne and events in Northumbria because Bede was such a reliable recounter of events in that area, based on his personal knowledge and first-hand accounts of colleagues. There were certainly other places where Irish Celt taught Anglo-Saxon (some of them duly mentioned by Bede but without the convincing wealth of detail he was able to paint of events within Northumbria itself). For example, Fursa established a monastery in Burgh castle, East Anglia, a Roman fort of the Saxon shore, some time in the 630s. Maeldubh founded the famous monastery of Malmesbury, where he taught Aldhelm (640–709), the first English scholar of any distinction. Dicuil, himself a pupil of Fursa, founded a monastery at Bosham, where a fine Saxon church stands today. Irish monks founded the great monastery of Abingdon in 685, "hardly second to any in England", and so on. And of course it was the Irish abbot Boisil who first taught Cuthbert, later to become venerated in Northumbria (Bede wrote his life), at the ancient foundation of Melrose in the Southern Uplands.

So the incredible had happened. Ireland succeeded where Rome had failed. England, a land of uncouth and warlike savages, became converted to Christianity and, eventually, civilised. That it was not all easy going may be deduced from a comment by Aldhelm in a letter to King Geraint of Dumnonia (Cornwall) mentioning that the Irish refused to eat from the same bowls as the English because of the latter's dirty habits, and insisted on having the bowls scoured before they used them! The English might never have become civilised at all: the first monk to be despatched from Iona at Oswald's request had given up and returned to Iona, announcing that he could make no headway with "an intractable people of stubborn and uncivilized character".

Now our story focuses again on Northumberland and the travels of two Northumbrian noblemen, Benedict Biscop (628–89) and Wilfrid (634–709). Each, as a relatively young man, became converted to Christianity, Wilfrid in time to study directly under Aidan at Lindisfarne. Each made several journeys to Rome, visiting en route such centres as Canterbury, Lérins, and Lyons. They were impressed. Benedict Biscop was to found the twin monasteries of Wearmouth and Jarrow and to richly endow them with a library of books brought from Europe, and thus incidentally equip Bede for his great work. They also brought back ideas of building in stone (substantial parts of Benedict Biscop's two monasteries remain), the use of glass, a school of sculpture, Roman church vestments, and plainsong in the Roman manner (later to be known as Gregorian Chant). They both thus came to admire and advocate Roman church practices.

These events inevitably brought the two churches, an authoritarian and organised Roman one, and the much looser Celtic one, into contact. In its evolution, the Roman church had had to deal painfully with a number of schismatic ideas, the outvoted dubbed as heresy and discarded, whatever might have been their intrinsic merit or even truth. Interestingly, a major and long-running heresy, eventually defeated at the

Council of Constantinople in 381 A.D., had been Arianism, which had gone some way towards the commonsense Unitarian view that Jesus was human and not divine. The Roman church was, one would have to say, a bit full of itself (some might say it still is). The Celtic church, on the other hand, one would have to admit, was individualistic and disorganised.

Contact was to turn into conflict. One import from Rome was to prove especially troublesome. This was due to the Roman church having altered the procedure for calculating the date of Easter during the period that the Celtic church was isolated from it. The problem was particularly acute for King Oswy of Northumbria. As a Celtic Christian, some years he found himself still in Lent while his wife, a Roman Christian convert from the south of England, was celebrating Easter! Other differences included the rites of baptism and the style of monk's tonsure (the Celts had adopted the druidical ear to ear tonsure, as opposed to the neat circular Benedictine one).

But Easter was the major stumbling block, and there was much, much more to it than simple differences in dates etc., annoying as these might have been. For the Roman Christians Easter signified the miracle of the resurrection and God's Grace to man, the doctrinal centrepiece of Christian faith in fact. For the Celts, always attuned to the natural world and to the human psyche, it was, at least in part, a time to give thanks for the seasonal rebirth of nature, and also a time for introspection and individual resolve, reminiscent of the eight-fold path of Buddhism.

Someone had to give. It is indicative of the importance of Northumbria at this time that an important

Synod to resolve differences was held not at Canterbury, but at Whitby. The fateful year was 664. Bede's account is riveting. The Roman advocate was the brash, well-travelled and eloquent Wilfrid. The Celtic one was the gentle, elderly, Iona-trained Colman, Abbot of holy Lindisfarne. Wilfrid's manner was that of a scornful prosecutor: why should "one remote corner of a remote island" impose itself on Rome was his rhetorical stance. King Oswy's adjudication was inevitable and final. Rome won the day. One can readily understand how the Celtic monks, who had achieved so much in their mission to England, felt aggrieved. Colman departed in a huff, first to Iona, and then on to Inishboffin, an island off the west coast of Mayo, where some of his monastic buildings remain, taking some (not all) of the Irish monks of Lindisfarne with him. God bless him and all the Irish who had travailed so, putting up with the uncouth English, their filthy eating bowls and all.

Northumbria quickly went on to accept the accoutrements of the Roman church. The formal acceptance of Roman Christianity and ongoing direct links with Rome and the continent further opened the floodgates to the legacy of the classical world in England. This went hand in hand with a revival of the rule of law, civil administration, development of currency, commerce, and town life. Prosperity, based on peace, was underpinned by increased population and the reclamation of new lands from forest assarts.

This Golden Age of Northumbria lasted from the second half of the 7th century through the 8th century. Its Irish-Germanic-Classical monastic culture became easily the greatest single achievement of post-Roman

Europe prior to the time of the Carolingian renaissance. The Northumbrian King Aldfrith (ruled 685–705) was the first literate king England had seen. He had studied in Ireland and even wrote poems in Irish. The new culture arose with amazing vigour from the fertile intermarriage of the idealism and zeal of the ascetic Irish, the energy of Germanic people and craftsmen, and the legacy of humanist learning from the classical world.

One unique masterpiece, showing this intermarriage in art form, has come down to us. This is the *Lindisfarne Gospels*, miraculously complete and intact, now housed in the British Museum. It is written in one hand, that of Bishop Eadfrith of Lindisfarne, and can be precisely dated to the last years of the 7th century. It is to my mind the greatest  work of its genre of the so-called Dark Ages. Compared to the Book of Kells (which certainly comes a close second; some may place it first), in the Lindisfarne Gospels equally supreme artistry is married with discipline.

A comparable work in stone is the awe-inspiring Ruthwell cross, another unique masterpiece, comparable to but differing in style from the Irish High Crosses. The Ruthwell Cross has bold figure carving (some of the figures are curiously reminiscent of Epstein's), intricate "Mediterranean" vine-leaf scroll inhabited with animals, and is margined by extracts from that most wonderful of all English poems, *The Song of the Rood*, written in runic characters. The Ruthwell cross and the similar, not far distant Bewcastle cross stand proudly athwart the two ancient overland routes, in part following Roman roads, that linked Northumbria to the Celtic Sea. The routes were well travelled and would have been well known, for example, to Columba's biographer Adamnan, abbot of Iona from 679 to 704, who made the return journey from Iona to Northumberland in 686 and again in 688. If travelling the southern route, no doubt he would have paused near Bewcastle Crags and gained heart for his journey from being able to see both Celtic and North Seas from this one spot.

Meanwhile, spreading southwards from Lindisfarne, a group of Anglian monks, who had been taught and inspired by Celts, carried the Christian message to the rest of England. Cedd converted the notorious East Saxons from a monastery at Bradwell-on-sea. Finan, who had succeeded Aidan as Abbot of Lindisfarne, managed to convert and baptize Peada, son of the great pagan Mercian King Penda. This landmark event is recorded in stone on the two Sandbach crosses in Cheshire. Chad, brother of Cedd and former pupil of Aidan, carried on this work in Mercia and adjacent areas from a foundation at Lichfield. Wilfrid, during a five-year period of exile (brought on by his own arrogant behaviour), converted the people of Sussex and the Isle of Wight.

Under the Christian aegis, a great deal of unification was thus accomplished in England. Theodore of Tarsus, Archbishop of Canterbury from 668 to 690, was able to convene the first council of the whole English church at Hertford in 673. He established a pattern of bishoprics that has endured with relatively minor modifications to the present day. This country-wide dialogue undoubtedly worked to bring to an end some of the tribal warfare of the past. Offa (ruled 757–96), for example, agreed or more likely imposed a clearly marked boundary between Mercia and Wales, effectively reducing squabbling over territory on the Celtic fringe.

But the story of the Irish monks of the Celtic church is not yet concluded. What had been achieved in England was paralleled on an even greater scale in western Europe, which witnessed a massive immigration of literate Irish monks, peaking in the 7th century. Some had been displaced from now Roman institutions in England. Many came fresh from Ireland. The saga is immense and cannot be fully told here.

Let us take Columbanus as an early example. Leaving Comgall's monastery at Bangor (Northern Ireland) in c.590, he set off for Europe with twelve companions and enjoyed mixed fortunes there. His first foundations were at Annegray, Luxeuil and Fontaine in the Vosges. After being expelled from Burgundy (for criticising the loose living of the royal family) he travelled down the Moselle and up the Rhine. Leaving Gall behind to found St. Gall, Columbanus crossed the Alps into Italy and founded Bobbio in the Appennines in the year 612 and died there in 615. St. Gall was to become a renowned seat of learning with a library described as being of "unsurpassed magnificence". Bobbio was to become easily the most important monastery in all Italy and possessor of a great scriptorium, producing for example manuscripts with the first carpet pages of intricate ornamentation. We know from his writings that Columbanus himself was familiar with many classical authors including Virgil, Horace, Ovid, and Eusebius. And so it went on. By the end of the 7th century there were over 400 monasteries in Gaul alone, the majority of them with Irish monks.

Subsequent generations of missionaries from the British Isles to the continent included English ones, inheritors of Celtic missionary traditions. With a more or less common language, still largely pagan Frisia and surrounding areas were plausible targets for the English missionaries. One of the first of these was Willibrord who successfully set up a bishopric in Utrecht in 695 and the renowned monastery of Echternach in Luxemburg a little later, where he died in 739. Others were less fortunate. For example, the two Hewards (English, but who had lived for some time in Ireland) were martyred in 695, and Wynfrith (aka Boniface) was killed in 754.

All this, and a great deal more, constituted a framework within which Celtic monks and their pupils worked to bring a decisive end to the Dark Age in Europe and set the scene for renaissance in the time of Charlemagne. Toynbee, for example, refers to the Irish classical scholar Erigena in these terms: "the giant of the Carolingian Renaissance whose like was not seen again in western Christendom until the Italian Renaissance of the fifteenth century."

Tragically, Lindisfarne itself, the original cradle of this part of our story, was to suffer repeated sackings in

Viking raids, including the very earliest in 793. The passage of centuries had possibly dulled Alcuin's sense of irony when he wrote later that year to King Ethelred of Northumbria:

> We and our fathers have now lived in this fair land for nearly 350 years and never before has such an atrocity been seen in Britain as we now have suffered at the hands of a pagan people.

But the seminal work of Lindisfarne had borne its fruit.

VII   LEGACY

I have a simple theory (I am told that it is not original but typically Celtic) and I believe the history of Britain illustrates it well: it is the *land* which tends to mould the character of a people, whatever accidents there may be of invaders and settlers. Britain offers a challenge in its climate and in the surrounding sea. This challenge encourages action, for it is a fair challenge. Nature is bounteous and the land is beautiful. Its people are pragmatic and tend to take things (including the weather!) as they come. They are strongly individualistic. They are fair. They are blessed. Britain made her Celts.

As a corollary to the above (and wearing for the moment the hat of a resource scientist), I have also come to realise with alarm that great danger today results from people losing contact with their natural environment. Man is a social animal, yes, but increasing numbers everywhere are now coming to live in an overcrowded, rootless, and meaningless urban world, governed by the artefact of money. Enormous extremes of wealth and poverty co-exist and are widening, and all too often they are not related either to the merits or to the needs of individuals. Society and the aims of society are grossly distorted by this. On a personal level, many now live part of their lives vicariously via TV and video and, to a corresponding degree, drop out of active participation in society. Some indulge in crime, others in venality, and still others in deviant behaviour comparable to that observed among overcrowded rats. All this becomes fodder for a mind-rotting but thriving gutter press.

Divorced from the natural world, it is also not surprising that so many remain tragically ignorant of Earth's fragile and eroding base of natural resources, which we take for granted and so recklessly plunder. At the present time, it can truly be said that we are existing in a materialistic fool's paradise. A fatal link has been forged between money, profit, and Earth's finite natural resources. In particular, we have become inescapably reliant on abundant and cheap energy sources that are, alas, in the main non-renewable and will become exhausted. Although this may soon prove to be the most stark element of a rapidly approaching predicament for humankind, it happens to be completely masked at the present time by a purely temporary glut of productive capacity for oil (our major energy source). But there are certainly grounds for deep concern over a great many other resource, environmental, social, and demographic issues.

And all the while, with the clock running against us, we are being misgoverned by what seem to be ignorant and patronising politicians. Although many of them might wish to remain men and women of integrity, increasingly they find themselve obliged to make their sales pitch to our own ignorance, baseness, and short-term greed (if they didn't the other side would). All this constitutes a vicious circle as dangerous as it is unedifying. The basic problem is that the noble ideal of democracy, to which all pay lip service, needs a reasonably educated and informed electorate that can sensibly and impartially consider major issues with the common good in mind. Instead of this ideal, politicians find the money to pay retainers well for all too effective advertising techniques of mind persuasion, much of it with the short-term profits of blind and amoral capitalism as a hidden agenda. Reliance is frequently put on the advice of economists, who, as Oscar Wilde once famously but aptly observed, know the price of everything and the value of nothing. Those who should be our secular leaders are thus effectively lacking in social purpose and certainly devoid of any informed thought for our long-term future. Many decent folk despair. All this surely invites disaster.

Furthermore, our major revealed religions, the essential message of their great prophets alas increasingly subverted and disfigured by ugly fundamentalisms, have to do mostly with the dubious Gnostic bribe of personal salvation for the righteous. They, too, thus have little or nothing to offer in the way of sensible ethical guidance on what has become a vital question: What are we doing to spaceship Earth's environment, life, and natural resources and hence to ourselves and to our own future?

> Take advice from him who makes you cry, not from him who makes you laugh.
>
> *Arab proverb*

What then, in view of this disturbing and developing scenario, as perceived by a growing minority at least, is so relevant and distinctive about the heroic age of the Celtic church and its legacy from so long ago that it should command our interest and respect at the present day?

That her Saints achieved a sustained saga without parallel of self-reliance, bravery, travel, and sheer scope of achievement with relatively very little in the way of resources is so dazzlingly apparent that it goes almost without saying – once one has rectified lacunae in traditional history books!

Then, as every teacher has to learn, along with the message is transmitted the messenger. It becomes a question not merely of what you teach, but what you are. All the more essential if you are a man of God. As we have seen, Bede, despite his honestly held genuine horror of the unorthodoxy of the Celtic church on what were to him some central matters of belief and practice, always spoke in the highest terms of the Irish monks themselves. As a further example, with his customary economy and precision, Bede wrote thus of Aidan: "The highest recommendation of his teaching to all was that he and his followers lived as they taught." I respect and echo Bede's epitaph.

Not for the Celtic saints of the heroic age chilling and childish depictions of hell and eternal damnation, and little for them of mortal sin and original sin. From the fragmentary records that we have, it seems that they spoke rather of the sweetness and beauty of this life on Earth in the sight of God. If you probe for shortcomings you will easily find them in us all. Better to look for and encourage the good in humankind. I find this supremely appealing – the essence of humanism, in fact.

We do know that the Celts put a very high value on education in its broadest sense. For example, the Celtic church preserved a unique native culture and, when the opportunity was given, it preserved and transmitted classical culture as well. How they would have revelled in the present-day extent of knowledge, particularly that of natural science and of the beauty and ramifications of Nature, which it is fashionable these days to refer to again as Gaia.

> To Gaia, mother of all of life and oldest of gods, I
>   sing,
> You who make and feed and guide all creatures of
>   the earth,
> Those who move on your firm and radiant land,
>   those who wing
> Your skies, those who swim your seas, to all these
>   you have given birth;
> Mistress, from you come all our harvests, our chil-
>   dren, our night and day,
> Yours the power to give us life, yours to take away.
> To you who contain everything,
> To Gaia, mother of all, I sing.
>   *Homeric Hymn to Earth*

By reasons of race-history and locale and contact with man's psychic roots, the people of the Celtic church were indeed always close to nature. God, as personified for them by Christ, was present for them in all their daily activities. Their Celtic inheritance encouraged them to continue with helpful principles for a *simple way of life in harmony with nature*.

Some of the above ideas and viewpoints can be seen

96

to be implicit in what has come to be known as the Pelagian heresy, destined to be combatted by Augustine (of Hippo) himself. Pelagius, who flourished around the turn of the 4th century, appears to us as the quintessential pragmatic Britisher. He was the first Britisher to make a lasting contribution to the cultural and religious life of Europe. He maintained that the grace of God was not for eliminating "original sin" (indeed, he appeared to seriously question the latter), but should be harnessed to guide our own life on earth. Furthermore, a God-fearing person is worthy of salvation by virtue of his or her own efforts. That was the heresy.

This may seem an overly subtle point until one thinks about it. Then one begins to realise the enormous stimulus, scope, and flexibility which a Pelagian/Celtic view of life provides for the harnessing of innate conscience, for individuality, for invention, for original thought, for effort, and thus for the formulation of changing priorities in our sadly changing world.

> All things in nature move and change and are renewed – nature never stands still.
> All thoughts and beliefs must also change – fixity of belief is against the life of the spirit.
> It is the spirit of endless quest that keeps alive and lively the mind of man – it is the spirit of free enquiry that brings "life" into the life of man – it is the spirit of free enquiry that brings about the spiritual growth of man.
>
> *Gábor Kereki* (Unitarian minister)

Finally, in this brief account of our Celtic legacy, we have scarcely mentioned that man, albeit not a saint but rather "once King and King to be", the man who may never even have lived, the man who had he lived were certainly mortal, the man who however lives for all time. The secret of the paradox is apparent when one thinks about it. Arthur has inspired Europe's greatest family of enduring legends quite simply because he represents the conscience which is present in each of us, including all those who have ever lived and the countless millions yet unborn. He has become for us the epitome of that appealing man, like each of us all too human, with certain strengths but all too vulnerable in his fraility and passions, who is personally driven to strive for the common good. For this reason it could be claimed that Arthur might be regarded as the greatest Christian Celt of all.

These then are what I believe to be some important components of the legacy of the Age of Saints. Their view of human existence could readily be extended today to include principles of *equity* and of *sustainability of natural resources* in our late-industrial society, i.e. the essential "ethical" dimensions of what might appear at first sight to be the merely "practical" problems that are now facing humanity, problems that alas are surely going to intensify.

Now no one should claim that the Celtic saints were some unique breed apart. They were not – that is the whole point of our common humanity, and this should be a source of encouragement to us. But they are ours, and we should cherish their legacy. Along with a growing number of "Celtic converts", I have come to believe therefore that this legacy, with its particular emphasis on individual conscience, can have considerable relevance

to us today. Of course, one can very usefully go on to meditate on the undoubted links between teachings and
ideas from such diverse sources as Buddhism, Celtic
Saints, St. Francis of Assisi, seekers in tolerant trad-
tions such as the Unitarians and Bahai, modern-day
Greens and so on.

Somewhere here, I strongly suspect, could be con-
structed both a rational philosophical base and a credi-
ble spiritual inspiration for our future, if we are to have
one. Somehow, we need to break the above-mentioned
vicious circle of ignorance, greed, and moral apathy. And
this process has to start with the individual. Where else?
What might have befallen the once uncouth English
without Aidan? What might befall us without renewed
understanding and faith? Who knows, perhaps an
understanding and love of Gaia will eventually come to
inspire those who may survive a terrible and inevitably
approaching Dark Age, just as a love of Christ once
unforgettably inspired those who faced, survived, and
eventually triumphed over a terrible Dark Age on the
Celtic Fringe of Europe.

Yes, it could be said that the saints of the Celtic Church
lost out to a disciplined and authoritarian Rome but, like
the Gododdin, they had earned their mead, and they
shall be honoured until the end of the world.

> Preserver of the faith,
> constant lover of his country,
> here lies Paulinus,
> the devoted champion of righteousness.
> *Translation of epitaph on an ancient stone,*
> *Carmarthen*

Sources

Contemporary written accounts of the Age of Saints are few indeed. True, some annals include reference to the period and some may well have had access to now lost earlier material, but they were penned centuries later and betray many lacunae and errors. To the evidence that can be gleaned from original written sources can, however, be added that of a significant number of archaeological remains and artefacts. The detective work involved in any synthesis is all really a matter for the specialist scholar, and has in turn spawned a large number of histories and commentaries. I should like therefore to refer to a highly condensed selection of material by reliable writers which I personally have found interesting and rewarding, and including, where it is possible, relatively inexpensive paperbacks. An alphabetic list of references follows later.

Beginning with tangible remains, Lloyd and Jennifer Laing's *Guide to Dark Age Remains in Britain* provides an interesting selection of accessible sites in England, Wales, and Scotland. Ireland is well catered for by two gazeteer guides, one by Estyn Evans, the other by Peter Harbison. Both usefully give grid references and both are prefaced by informatory introductions. I have found that in the field one often usefully complements the other. Chris Barber's two popular and well-illustrated books on mysterious Wales include interesting sites with precise grid references, arranged by topics such as crosses and holy wells (although some may think he goes over the top by including material on ley-lines, wizards, and sunken cities). Janet and Colin Bord's *Mysterious Britain* (the first of a stable of similar books by them) covers both Britain and Ireland in a comparable vein. Nash-Williams is an authoritative reference source for ancient Welsh inscribed stone monuments. Leslie Alcock has the happy knack of presenting scholarship intelligibly, and brilliantly integrates archaeological with documentary evidence for Dark-Age Britain excluding Ireland. Although, as mentioned, the enigmatic Picts are peripheral to our story, an excellent short account of them (and the evidence is almost entirely archaeological) is given by Anna Ritchie. Of course, much material of archaeological interest ends up in museums, notably the British Museum, London, the Royal Museum of Scotland, Edinburgh, the National Museum of Wales, Cardiff, the Manx Museum, Douglas, and the National Museum of Ireland, Dublin. The latter houses a truly magnificent collection of Dark-Age artefacts. These museums and many other major sites also have well-stocked bookshops which can prove happy hunting grounds for material to add to one's library.

Part of our story has had to do with the carry-over of Celtic ways into Christian times. For insights into the early Celts we are fortunate in having several excellent books. Peter Beresford Ellis documents "the first millennium of Celtic history" ending with Caesar's invasion of Britain. T. G. E. Powell's well-illustrated book remains a classic. Peter Harbison documents pre-Christian Ireland "from first settlers to the early Celts". Miranda Green tells of the Gods of the Celts, and Jeffrey Gantz provides an accessible source of a collection of early Irish myths and sagas. Among many interesting titles, the Shire Archaeology series includes Ruth and Vincent Megaw's *Early Celtic Art in Britain and Ireland*, while the Paladin Archaeological History series includes Lloyd Laing's *Celtic Britain* (excluding Ireland but spanning both pre-Roman and post-Roman time).

An authoritative and recently updated text on Roman times in Britain is Peter Salway's *Roman Britain*, while the same author's *Oxford Illustrated History of Roman Britain* is probably more appealing for the general reader. A useful gazeteer is Shire Publication's *Discovering Roman Britain* edited by David E. Johnston. Leonard Cottrell's delightful account of an itinerary he made following Roman roads to Roman towns is hugely enjoyable. Another Paladin title, apposite to our theme, is Stephen Johnson's account of later Roman Britain. Charles Thomas's scholarly *Christianity in Roman Britain to AD 500* is an invaluable discussion of available evidence, usefully overlapping from late Roman times into the early Dark Ages.

We must now address the thorny question of sources of information on the Dark Ages. Hardinge summarises early histories, narratives, saints' lives, glosses (for example, insertions in Irish on copied Latin texts), poems, and annals. The above-mentioned Leslie

Alcock discusses in detail the contribution and reliability of the main sources. We are fortunate indeed in
having the 5th-century *Confesio* and *Epistola* of
Patrick. The *Confesio* is a personal statement by
Patrick of his mission to the Irish, including a confes-
sion of gratitude to God for sending him on that mission. The *Epistola* is an angry letter addressed to the
British king Corotius who had unkindly imprisoned
and butchered some Irish Christians. *The Ruin of
Britain* by Gildas is our only surviving first-hand
account of turbulent times in Britain in the 5th and
early 6th centuries. It was written during what seems
to have been a discernible lull in warfare between English and British around the second quarter of the 6th
century. Viewed as an historical document, it is frus-
tratingly short on precise names and dates. Much of it
is a polemic against the abuses of several contemporary clerics and princes. Nevertheless, it is priceless.
The Life of Samson of Dol, translated by T. Taylor, was
compiled by an anonymous monk around 615, some
fifty years after Samson's death in 565. He was able to
draw on source material given to him by an octogenar-
ian nephew of deacon Henod, himself a cousin of Samson. Adamnan wrote his *Life of Columba* some
hundred years after the latter's death in 597 while he
too was an abbot of Iona from 679 to 704. Bede's magnificent *History of the English Church and People* was
completed in 731, a little later than his *Life of Cuthbert*
(who had died in 687 and of whom many of Bede's older
colleagues would have had personal knowledge) and
his *Lives of the Abbots of Wearmouth and Jarrow*
(whom Bede knew personally). The Penguin editions of
the *History* and *Lives* have extended introductions

103

which are very well worth reading. The *British History* of Nennius, compiled around A.D. 800 from miscellanous older manuscripts, is another frustrating document. Nennius tells us that he made a heap of all the material he had at his disposal and put it together. The result is fragmentary but fascinating – it contains, for example, the first historical allusion to Arthur (apart from what is possibly the Dark Age's greatest throwaway line, occurring in the Gododdin: "But he was no Arthur"). Nevertheless, it is clearly based on genuine older accounts. Translations with commentaries of Patrick, Gildas, and Nennius are available in softback from Phillimore. *The Mabinogion*, translated by and with an introduction by Jeffrey Gantz, although it provides fascinating glimpses into Celtic mythology, is based on material of which our earliest complete copy is in the *Red Book of Hergest*, dating from c.1400. The *Anglo-Saxon Chronicles*, translated by Anne Savage, first compiled by unknown monks writing in several monasteries and beginning in the 9th century, are understandably short on material directly to do with the Celtic regions, but provide an independent and corroborative time-frame for events as seen from the English side.

Histories and commentaries about the Age of Saints, i.e. "secondary sources", as opposed to the above-mentioned sparse and diverse primary sources, are numerous. One of the most comprehensive and well referenced is John Morris's *The Age of Arthur: A History of the British Isles from 350 to 650*. Charles Thomas's *Celtic Britain* (referring to post-Roman times) and *Britain and Ireland in Early Christian Times, A.D. 400–800* are praiseworthy examples of a scholar writing accurate and popular books. Richard Muir is a most readable contemporary writer on Britain's history and countryside. His well-illustrated *Dark Age and Medieval Britain* includes interesting early chapters with evocative titles: "Into an age of darkness", "Christianity the path back to civilization", and "The Dark Age countryside – a mystery tour". Other readable texts with self-explanatory titles are Leslie Hardinge's *The Celtic Church in Britain* and Nora Chadwick's *The Age of Saints in the Early Celtic Church*. E. G. Bowen in his *The Settlements of the Celtic Saints in Wales* brilliantly assesses the Welsh evidence as far as it can reasonably be taken. A comparable service is provided by Maire and Liam De Paor's *Early Christian Ireland*. Bowen, in his *Saints, Seaways, and Settlements*, documents the ongoing maritime tradition of the Celtic peoples. The same theme is taken up, with particular reference to the coming of Christianity to Scotland, by Daphne Pochin-Mould and, most recently, by John Marsden. Contemporary events on the English side are documented by Collingwood and Myers in their *Roman Britain and the English Settlements*.

Regarding the saints themselves, *Lives of the British Saints* by Baring-Gould and Fisher includes, inter alia, interesting material on Beuno, Brychan, Cadoc, Cybi, Deiniol, Gildas, Illtyd, Padarn, Paulinus, and Seiriol, but it is based mainly on writings penned centuries later than the events described, and much of it must be considered as of doubtful veracity. The same criticism applies to *Lives of the Welsh Saints* by Doble, including those of Dubricius, Illtyd, and Paulinus. The cited edition has a long and useful introductory chapter on "our early Welsh saints and history". Compendiums of biographies of saints (always bearing in mind the widely differing degrees of reliability of sources) include the *Penguin Dictionary of Saints* by Donald Attwater, two books by Daphne Pochin-Mould on *Irish Saints* and *Celtic Saints*, and a useful chronological account of the *Saints of Ireland* by Mary Ryan D'Arcy.

For the extended mission of the Celtic church to England and beyond, useful sources are the books with self-explanatory titles by Henry Mayr-Harting and Margaret Gallyon, and the two books by Peter Beresford Ellis, *Celt and Saxon* (subtitled *The Struggle for Britain A.D. 410–937*) and *Celtic Inheritance* (including valuable details of the European scene of activity of Celtic monks).

For information on the artistic and cultural legacy of the Age of Saints, a useful starting point is *Early Christian Irish Art* by Francoise Henry. Lloyd Laing's *Later Celtic Art* documents a continuity from before to after the Golden Age of the 7th and 8th centuries. A wider view of art and society is provided by Lloyd and Jennifer Laing's *Art and Society in Celtic Britain and Ireland*. Dillon and Chadwick's *Celtic Realms* contains good chapters on Celtic art and literature. Matthew Arnold's *On the Study of Celtic Literature* is learned and still readable despite having been written over a century ago. Its publication, incidentally, was instrumental in the setting up of a Chair of Celtic at Oxford in spite of patronising opposition from classical scholars. Books on more specific themes include Malcolm Seaborne's book on crosses and Derek Bryce's *Symbolism of the Celtic Cross*. Janet Backhouse includes a selection of 24 pages in colour of the magnificent *Lind-*

isfarne Gospels, plus a full account of its history and setting. Peter Brown similarly includes 48 colour pages of the equally magnificent *Book of Kells*, plus an informative introduction.

In a more reflective vein, John Ferguson combines a biography of Pelagius with a discussion of the philosophical (heretical!) implications of Pelagianism. Shirley Toulson's *The Celtic Alternative* is subtitled *A Reminder of the Christianity we lost*. A much-quoted short article by Lynn White, 'The Historical Roots of our Ecological Crisis', that appeared some years ago in the magazine *Science*, is also very much in line with the theme of this book. It refers to the ideas of St. Francis in expressing "an alternative Christian view of man and nature". As for the enduring Arthur, let us be content with Gwyn William's exploration and discussion in *Excalibur*, which accompanied the TV series of that name. Shirley Toulson's *Celtic Journeys* is a travelogue and commentary on Celtic sites, mainly in Scotland, and including the cradles of Iona and Lindisfarne. If one is fortunate enough to have the opportunity to visit Lindisfarne, then Magnus Magnusson's *Lindisfarne* should go with one.

Some of the above contain excellent fuller bibliographies, notably recent books by Ellis, Laing and Laing, Marsden, and Thomas.

Epilogue

As well as following a well-trodden highroad provided by conventional written sources, one can recommend another all-important source of understanding, already strongly hinted at: namely, a meandering green path of personal travel and exploration in Celtic lands. So, if you will, perhaps with a few selected paperbacks in your rucksack, set your face to the west wind, and Go! Wander. Explore. Linger. Rest your spirit. Return whenever you can, be it in mind or body, and be refreshed. A pilgrimage undertaken anywhere within our precious Celtic Fringe will never be in vain. And you will slowly come to realise and then remember all your life that the Age of Saints can speak directly to the mind and the soul of the individual, to each one of us.

A Celtic Blessing

Deep peace of the running wave to you,
Deep peace of the flowing air to you,
Deep peace of the quiet earth to you,
Deep peace of the shining stars to you,
Deep peace of the Son of Peace to you.

References

Adamnan. *Life of Saint Columba, Founder of Hy (Iona)*, W. Reeves, 1856, facsimile reprint, Llanerch Press, 1990.

Alcock, L. *Arthur's Britain: History and Archaeology A.D. 367–634*, Penguin Books, 1971.

Arnold, M. *On the Study of Celtic Literature*, 1867; Everyman's Library edition with introduction by Ernest Rhys, 1905.

Attwater, D. *The Penguin Dictionary of Saints*, 2nd edition revised by Catherine Rachel John, Penguin Books, 1983.

Backhouse, J. *The Lindisfarne Gospels*, Phaidon, 1981.

Barber, C. *Mysterious Wales*, Granada, 1983.

Barber, C. *More Mysterious Wales*, Granada, 1987.

Baring-Gould, S. & Fisher, J. *Lives of the British Saints*, edited by Derek Bryce, Llanerch Press, 1990.

Bede. *Life of Cuthbert* and *Lives of the Abbots of Wearmouth and Jarrow*, in The Age of Bede, translated by J. F. Webb, edited and with Introduction by D. H. Farmer, reprinted with revisions, Penguin Books, 1988.

Bede. *A History of the English Church and People*, translated by Leo Sherley-Price, revised edition, Penguin Classics, 1968.

Bord, J., & Bord, C. *Mysterious Britain*, Grafton, 1974.

Bowen, E. G. *The Settlements of the Celtic Saints in Wales*, University of Wales Press, 1954.

Bowen, E. G. *Saints, Seaways and Settlements in the Celtic Lands*, University of Wales Press, 2nd edition, 1977.

Brown, P. *The Book of Kells*, Thames and Hudson, 1980.

Bryce, D. *Symbolism of the Celtic Cross*, Llanerch Press, 1989.

Chadwick, N. K. *The Age of Saints in the Early Celtic Church*, Oxford University Press, 1961.

REFERENCES

Collingwood, R. G. & Myres, J. N. L. *Roman Britain and the English Settlements*, Oxford University Press, 1937.

Cottrell, L. *Seeing Roman Britain*, revised edition, Pan Books, 1967.

D'Arcy, M. R. *The Saints of Ireland*, Irish American Cultural Institute, Minnesota, 3rd edition, 1985.

De Paor, M. & De Paor, L. *Early Christian Ireland*, Thames & Hudson, 1958.

Dillon, M. & Chadwick, N. *The Celtic Realms*, Weidenfeld & Nicolson, 1967.

Doble, G. H. *Lives of the Welsh Saints* (edited by D. Simon Evans), University of Wales Press, Cardiff, 1971.

Durant, G. M. Britain, *Rome's most northerly province: A History of Roman Britain, A.D. 43–A.D. 450*, G. Bell & Sons, 1970.

Ellis, P. B. *The Celtic Empire: The First Millennium of Celtic History c.1000 B.C.–51 A.D.*, Guild Publishing, 1990.

Ellis, P. B. *Celtic Inheritance*, Constable, 1992.

Ellis, P. B. *Celt and Saxon: The Struggle for Britain A.D. 410–937*, BCA, 1993.

Evans, E. *Prehistoric and Early Christian Ireland: A Guide*, Batsford, 1966.

Ferguson, J. *Pelagius: A Historical and Theological Study*, Heffer & Sons, 1956.

Gallyon, M. *The Early Church in Northumbria*, Terrence Dalton, 1977.

Gantz, J. *The Mabinogion*, Penguin Classics, 1976.

Gantz, J. *Early Irish Myths and Sagas*, Penguin Classics, 1981.

Gildas. *The Ruin of Britain* and other documents, translated and edited by M. Winterbottom, Phillimore, 1978.

Green, M. *The Gods of the Celts*, Alan Sutton, 1986.

Harbison, P. *Guide to the National Monuments in the Republic of Ireland*, Gill & Macmillan, 1970.

Harbison, P. *Pre-Christian Ireland from the First Settlers to the Early Celts*, Thames and Hudson, 1988.

Hardinge, L. *The Celtic Church in Britain*, S.P.C.K., 1972.

Henry, H. *Early Christian Irish Art*, Mercier Press, Cork, 3rd edition, 1979.

Johnson, S. *Later Roman Britain*, Grafton Books, 1982.

113

Johnston, D. E. *Discovering Roman Britain*, Shire Publications, revised edition, 1993.

Laing, L. *Celtic Britain*, Grafton, 1981.

Laing, L. *Later Celtic Art in Britain and Ireland*, Shire Publications, 1987.

Laing, L. & Laing, J. *A Guide to the Dark Age Remains in Britain*, Constable, 1979.

Laing, L. & Laing, J. *Celtic Britain and Ireland: Art and Society*, BCA, 1995.

Magnusson, M. *Lindisfarne: The Cradle Island*, Oriol Press, 1984.

Marsden, J. *Sea-Road of the Saints; Celtic Holy Men in the Hebrides*, Floris Books, 1995.

Mayr-Harting, H. *The Coming of Christianity to Anglo-Saxon England*, Batsford, 3rd edition, 1991.

Megaw, R. & Megaw, V. *Early Celtic Art in Britain and Ireland*, Shire Publications, 1990.

Morris, J. *The Age of Arthur: A History of the British Isles from 350 to 650*, Phillimore, 1977.

Muir, R. *Dark Age and Medieval Britain 400–1350*, George Philip, 1985.

Nash-Williams, V. E. *The Early Christian Monuments of Wales*, University of Wales Press, 1957.

Nennius. *British History*, edited and translated by John Morris, Phillimore, 1980.

Patrick. *Confesio* and *Epistola,* plus Muirchu's Life, translated and edited by A. B. E. Hood, Phillimore, 1978.

Pochin-Mould, D. C. *Scotland of the Saints*, Batsford, 1952.

Pochin-Mould, D. C. *The Celtic Saints*, Macmillan, 1956.

Pochin-Mould, D. C. *The Irish Saints*, Clonmore & Reynolds, Dublin, 1964.

Powell, T. G. E. *The Celts*, Thames and Hudson, new softback edition, 1983.

Ritchie, A. *Picts*, HMSO, 1989.

Salway, P. *Roman Britain*, Oxford University Press, 1981.

Salway, P. *Oxford Illustrated History of Roman Britain*, Oxford University Press, 1993.

Savage, A. *The Anglo-Saxon Chronicles*, Macmillan Papermac, 1984.

Seaborne, M. *Celtic Crosses of Britain and Ireland*, Shire Publications, 1989.

Taylor, T. *The Life of St. Samson of Dol*, facsimile reprint of 1925 S.P.C.K. edition, Llanerch Press, 1991.

Thomas, C. *Britain and Ireland in Early Christian Times A.D. 400–800*, Thames & Hudson, 1971.

Thomas, C. *Christianity in Roman Britain to A.D. 500,* Batsford, 1985.

Thomas, C. *Celtic Britain*, Thames & Hudson, 1986.

Toulson, S. *Celtic Journeys*, Hutchinson, 1985.

Toulson, S. *The Celtic Alternative: A Reminder of the Christianity we lost*, Rider, 1987.

White, L. 'The Historical Roots of our Ecologic Crisis', *Science*, vol. 155, pp. 1203–1207, 1967.

Williams, G. *Excalibur: The Search for Arthur*, BBC Books, 1994.